FLORALIA

The University of North Carolina Press, Chapel Hill, N. C.; The Baker and Taylor Company, New York; Oxford University Press, London; Maruzen-Kabushiki-Kaisha, Tokyo; Edward Evans & Sons, Ltd., Shanghai; D. B. Centen's Wetenschappelijke Boekhandel, Amsterdam

EDWARD'S ORANGE LILY

FLORALIA

GARDEN PATHS AND BY-PATHS
OF THE EIGHTEENTH CENTURY
By JUNE RAINSFORD BUTLER

Chapel Hill
THE UNIVERSITY
of North Carolina
PRESS

COPYRIGHT, 1938, BY
THE UNIVERSITY OF NORTH CAROLINA PRESS

PJ

THIS EDITION IS LIMITED TO 500 COPIES,
AND THE TYPE FROM WHICH IT WAS PRINTED
HAS BEEN MELTED.

For

MY FAMILY

PREFACE

GARDEN PATHS AND BY-PATHS of the eighteenth century, like all paths and by-paths that ever were, had reasons for being. Some of these paths had insignificant beginnings in preceding centuries. Many of them were opened up and pushed on by men who were pioneers in an undeveloped field of science or in some new phase of the more practical aspects of gardening. Frequently the paths came upon obstacles that could not be surmounted, and as a result interesting by-paths were sent out in new directions. These new paths spread in interest and purpose, and, curiously enough, by following them, one can study the social and political as well as the horticultural changes of an age that advanced very rapidly.

As the eighteenth century afforded leisure for artistic expression in which gardening served as a medium, so now in this twentieth century, which is bringing increasing leisure, there is a manifestation of renewed interest in gardens. It is my wish that *Floralia*, which gives an account of some of the horticultural endeavors of two hundred years ago, will aid gardeners today worthily to reflect their finer spirits through garden activities.

PREFACE

I wish to express my appreciation to The Garden Club of America for permission to use that part of Chapter IX on the *Camellia japonica* which has been published in their Bulletin; to *Country Life* for permission to use the article on Pierre Joseph Redouté; to Gordon Dunthorne for his reading of the manuscript for factual accuracy; to Anne Ketchin Murph for her interest and help; to Rosa M. Wade for her help in transcribing notes and for the final typing of the manuscript; to all those members of the staff of the Library of Congress and of the Library of the Department of Agriculture who aided in assembling the materials which made this book.

JUNE RAINSFORD BUTLER

Edgefield, South Carolina
July 8, 1938

FOREWORD

By Gordon Dunthorne

THE FULL ENJOYMENT of a garden is not confined merely to the out-of-doors, but all the year round it can be a source of endless pleasure to those who are interested in its history and literature, tracing the sources of transitions and changes in design, appearing in one country later to affect another, the history and provenance of our favorite flowers of today, the lives of the pioneers both naturalists and explorers, who first discovered these flowers and brought them to Europe from all parts of the world.

The more we read and learn of its past the more we shall enjoy our gardens today, as this flower or that will be not only lovely for its color, form, and fragrance but there may be romance in its history and discovery.

Mrs. Butler's book does much to open our eyes to the varied activities of the eighteenth century and its important contribution to garden history, and tells delightfully of its personalities. *Floralia* should start many on the quest for further perusal of the garden literature of this fascinating century.

CONTENTS

	Foreword, by Gordon Dunthorne	ix
I.	Some Paths and By-paths	1
II.	The Rise of English Landscape Gardening	19
III.	A Company of English Gardeners	35
IV.	Noble Patrons of the Gentle Art	51
V.	America: A Floral Hunting Ground	70
VI.	Worthy Volumes about Trees	94
VII.	William Curtis: The Founder of the *Botanical Magazine*	110
VIII.	Pierre Joseph Redouté: The Raphael of Flowers	126
IX.	A Medley of Blossoms	138
X.	"Rose! Thou Art the Sweetest Flower"	152
	Bibliography	167
	Index	179

ILLUSTRATIONS

Edward's Orange Lily	*Frontispiece*
Portrait of Linnaeus	6
An Eighteenth-Century Garden	22
Title Page of *Catalogus Plantarum*	38
Portrait of Sir Hans Sloane	54
Crimson Pennsylvania Martagon	76
Portrait of William Curtis	112
A Plan of the Botanic Garden at Brompton	117
Redouté's Dahlia	132
One of Redouté's Roses	152

FLORALIA

"You must know, Sir, that I look upon the Pleasure which we take in a Garden, as one of the innocent Delights in human life. A Garden was the Habitation of our first Parents before the Fall. It is naturally apt to fill the mind with Calmness and Tranquility, and to lay all its turbulent Passions at rest. It gives us a great Insight into the Contrivance and Wisdom of Providence, and suggests innumerable subjects for Meditation. I cannot but think the very Complacency and Satisfaction which a man takes in these Works of Nature, to be a laudable, if not a virtuous Habit of Mind."—*The Spectator,* September 6, 1712.

CHAPTER I

Some Paths and By-Paths

IN THE SMALL VILLAGE OF RASHULT IN THE province of Småland, Sweden, on May 23, 1707, was born to Nils Linnaeus, the rector of the village, and his wife, Christina Broderson, a son who was called Charles. Though his ancestors came of peasant stock, some of his relatives, who had quitted the plough for more elevated pursuits in years that had passed, changed their family name with their profession; they borrowed the names of Lindelius or Tiliander, from a lofty linden tree, which stood at the time in the vicinity of their native place, between Tomsbodo and Linnhult. This custom of taking a new surname from a natural object was not an unusual one in Sweden. The father of Linnaeus, as the first learned man of his family, could not withstand following the example which his kindred had set before him. He likewise borrowed of the same tree a name which his son afterwards made immortal in every quarter of the globe.

While still quite young, Charles evidenced the fact that he had inherited his father's singular love of gardening.

FLORALIA *Some Paths and By-Paths*

Although this fond parent felt disappointment that his son did not show an early predilection for the ministry, he was more than willing to indulge him in his love of nature, trusting that with the boy's development ready shoulders would receive the parental mantle. Young Charles was sent to Wexicoe to a Latin school for instruction, which, it was hoped, would qualify him for his future clerical vocation. At every step in life, Charles Linnaeus evidently felt called more closely into the intimate folds of nature. Instead of becoming a serious ministerial student at Wexicoe, he became somewhat of a truant vagabond and spent all the time he could take or steal from ecclesiastical matters in making excursions into the surrounding fields and woods to collect bees and wasps, flowers and ferns, or anything that related to his beloved work.

All admonitions for a closer application to theology were in vain. His professors complained to his father that the Goddess Flora reigned supreme in young Charles's life and that he apparently felt little obligation to the "dogmatical acquirements," the Hebrew language, and the other solid branches of scholastic learning. Disappointed, mortified, and overwhelmed by his sense of helplessness, Nils Linnaeus resolved to make his son leave school and to apprentice him to an honest shoemaker and cobbler.

The physician to the Wexicoe School, John Rothmann, a nature lover himself, and by mere chance acquainted with Charles, understood the propensities of this student. He was struck by the spirit of penetration and unusual knowledge in one so young. It was he who prevailed upon the irate father to permit the boy to return to school and pursue such studies in natural history as would eventually lead to a degree of Doctor of Medicine. Rothmann placed in the hands of the young pupil, whose cause he had championed, the principal work of Tournefort, published in Paris in 1694, entitled *Élémens de botanique*. Linnaeus afterwards said that this book became the torch which illuminated the path of his youth and opened new avenues for his eager view; it was, at the same time, the source of the inspiration which he received and later handed on to his disciples. This book changed his point of view and helped him understand nature and her work of creation in a way impossible for him before. It is, therefore, to the then attending physician of the Wexicoe School that the world of science owes a debt for help in shaping one of the greatest botanists of all time.

The more Linnaeus knew of the wonders of his goddess, the more enthusiastically he studied these wonders, and during the years in attendance at the University of Upsala, which he entered in 1728, his superior knowledge and aptitudes in this field in a large measure compensated for the slender state of his finances. His professors in natural science were Olaud Rudbeck and Lars Roberg, both old men. Although he enjoyed his studies and work in the botanical garden, where he was made assistant to Professor Rudbeck in 1730, he was almost overwhelmed many times by the adverse conditions circumscribing his

FLORALIA *Some Paths and By-Paths*

life. Few men who have achieved eminence had a tougher struggle with dire poverty, but nature seems to have a way of preserving her own. At the most acute point in this needy period, Linnaeus found spiritual and material sustenance in the newly made friendship of Olaf Celsius, whom he considered the only true botanist of that day in Sweden. This friendship was the outcome of a casual visit made by Celsius to the botanical garden; the extensive knowledge of the young man who acted as his guide so profoundly impressed Celsius that he made inquiries about him. When informed of the ability, as well as the distress of Linnaeus, he offered him a home and congenial work. One of Charles's duties was to collect information for a very learned volume which his benefactor was writing; in this way he had access to the library of Celsius, one of the richest and most valuable in Sweden in botanical works. In addition he had the instruction and advice of the great man for whom he worked. For the remainder of his life, Linnaeus, who had many benefactors, valued Celsius as the greatest personality and influence of them all.

In 1732 at the age of twenty-five Linnaeus was sent by the Academy of Sciences on a collecting trip of over five thousand miles through Lapland. For the journey, a difficult and disagreeable one, he was given only a small amount of money and afterwards spoke of it as being particularly toilsome; "and I own that I was obliged to sustain more hardships and dangers in this sole peregrination through the frontier of our northern world, than in all the travels which I undertook in other parts, though

FLORALIA *Some Paths and By-Paths*

not without fatigue and weariness." He published the results of this trip in *Flora Lapponica.*

Revolutionizing work and activities filled the life of the young scientist; honor was the result of some of it but often the result was violent conflict with contemporary naturalists, for "revolutions are never effected in the bosom of peace and perfect concordance." Linnaeus gave several years to study and writing with trips in between. In 1735 he received his degree of Doctor of Medicine at the University of Harderwyk in Holland. It was customary in Sweden for students to take their degrees in foreign universities, a fashion which, if conducive to a broader erudition, was rather expensive. Linnaeus, on whom fortune smiled in critical moments, received some money for the undertaking from the girl to whom he was betrothed. In the same year there appeared at Leyden one of his earliest works, *Systema Naturae.* In it are tables giving a systematic grouping of the three natural kingdoms—minerals, plants, and animals. Linnaeus's division of plants into twenty-four classes, determined mainly by the number or some other obvious character of the stamens, is known as the sexual system. The next year his even more important work, *Genera Plantarum,* was published and this revolutionized classification. Linnaeus returned to Stockholm in 1738, where he settled down to the practice of medicine. However, in 1741, he was called to the University of Upsala; here he spent the rest of his days as a professor, first of medicine, and later of botany. In 1761 he was knighted and from that time he was called

FLORALIA *Some Paths and By-Paths*

Carl von Linné. On January 10, 1778, he died at the age of 70 years, 7 months and 17 days.

Linnaeus is accorded a place as an outstanding naturalist, primarily because of the clear system of classification which he worked out, and also because of the stimulus he gave to further accomplishment along the same line. Those who followed him felt his influence and gave more attention to the study of the structure of plants; they learned the importance of the various parts and organs. Prior to that time the male plants had been considered useless and had often been thrown out because they did not bear fruit.

Although scientific classification of plants reached a climax in the accomplishments of the great Linnaeus, he had benefited by the work of others, much of it gropingly done. Before the middle of the seventeenth century botany had been a chaos of unarranged fact and ill classified material; during the late 1600's, a definite upbuilding had begun. Malpighi in Italy, Tournefort in France, and John Ray in England were among those who labored at bringing about some ordered arrangement. Concerning Ray, George Johnson in his *History of English Gardening* says: "Indefatigable, enthusiastick in his pursuits, of clear and comprehensive mind, he gave an impetus to Botany and its correllative Arts, more effectual to their advancement than they had received during ages of years preceeding. For fifty years he most successfully laboured to clear the path of the Science and to increase her stores. Nor does he enjoy his fame only among his country-men,

CHARLES LINNAEUS

FLORALIA *Some Paths and By-Paths*

it is afforded to him by all Europe." Ray was responsible for giving significance to relationship of offspring and ancestors in the plant world, though unfortunately the importance of these factors was scarcely comprehended at the time. Ray's work, added to that which had been done in this field for a century, prepared the way for the great Swedish botanist.

One of the most important paths which led to a general awakening in the field of natural history was the scientific classification of plants, for certainly during the eighteenth century horticulture in all its branches made rapid strides. In addition to the botanists and their valuable work, there was also a group of chemists who were especially interested in horticulture, and through their researches knowledge was gained about plant food and soils and the part played by air, heat and light. It is not at all surprising that horticulture advanced so rapidly since the scientific men of the time applied the results of their researches to the plant world and its inhabitants.

In striking contrast to Linnaeus with his original work was Richard Bradley, who drew quite heavily on contemporary gardeners for his information instead of making his own discoveries. His writings devote considerable space to the budding of trees, to bulbs, and to methods of obtaining double flowers and variegated forms. In advising when to graft he evidently was influenced by John Evelyn, for he said: "The New Moon and Old Wood are best." He was also much concerned with the fertilization of plants and the movement of sap. Not only did Bradley write of the activities of his contemporaries, but he delved into volumes of the past, and put his findings in such shape that the men of his own generation had the benefit of the work of the horticulturists who had preceded them. He not only made the information gleaned from books readily available, but he carried on a voluminous correspondence with men of learning in the scientific world, and he was generous in putting whatever information he acquired at the disposal of those who were feeling their way along by their own efforts.

Bradley's energy and enthusiasm, which accomplished so much that was beneficial to his co-laborers, carried him far afield. The Royal Society recognized him and his work and made him a Fellow. Afterwards he was elected professor of botany at Cambridge, which honor, according to an early account, he obtained in a dishonorable and clandestine manner. Although this position gave him prestige and was responsible for a wide circulation of his writings, he neglected the duties of his professorship and behaved in such a dissolute manner that he would have been deprived of his position if death had not come unexpectedly in 1732.

One of Bradley's contemporaries was John Lawrence, a rector, who spent the last ten years of his life, 1722-1732, as a prebendary of Salisbury after having served many parishes. He was a naturalist and prided himself upon the very fine fruits that he cultivated. Working in his garden was his greatest pleasure, and he says it was "the best and almost only physick" he took. Mr. Lawrence published the

FLORALIA *Some Paths and By-Paths*

following: *The Gentlemen's Recreation* in 1714, *The Lady's Recreation in the Art of Gardening* in 1717, and *The Clergyman's Recreation* in 1726. The contents of these books, the results of many years of practical observation and experience, were so excellent that John Lawrence was ranked among the great writers of the time on horticultural subjects.

Lawrence and Bradley were interested in the practical value of methods of forcing. In his *Works of Nature,* 1724, Bradley wrote: "Take notice, that during the cold season, when these Fruits are forced to shoot unseasonably, the Plants must be cover'd with glasses to prevent the injuries they might receive from frosts." John Lawrence, in his *Fruit Garden Kalendar,* cited an account of an early example of forcing; he says in 1718 he heard that the Duke of Rutland at Belvoir Castle in Lincolnshire hastened his grapes by having fires burning from Lady-day to Michaelmas behind his sloped walls, a report which he evidently did not believe but which "it is easy to conceive."

The greenhouse, essential for experimentation, had an interesting evolution. During the seventeenth century a type of unheated structure had been used, but forcing of plants was almost unknown at that time. Contributing to the development of the greenhouse was Nicholas Facio Duilhier, who was born in Switzerland in 1664, and who came over to England in 1687. Because of his success as a teacher of mathematics and his general accomplishments he was made a Fellow in the Royal Society. Alive to the prevailing interest in gardening he wrote: *Fruit Walls, im-*

FLORALIA *Some Paths and By-Paths*

proved by inclining them to the Horizon: or a way to build walls for Fruit trees where they may receive more sunshine and heat than ordinary. Led by his studies in mathematics to the writing of this work, published in London in 1699, using its principles and the laws of optics, he demonstrates the advantage of receiving rays of heat and light at right angles. In Bradley's *Gentleman and Gardener's Kalendar,* which was published in 1718, there is a very interesting drawing which depicts the fruit wall. The walls alone were found to be less effective than had been anticipated. The next development was to cover the space between the two walls with glass and the final result took place in 1724 when the first greenhouse in England was erected at the Oxford Physic Garden.

The advantages of the hothouse were readily apparent and promptly accepted. Thinking with enthusiasm of some flowering winter plants he wished to cultivate for his diversion, John Bartram wrote to Peter Collinson in a letter dated June 24, 1760, "I am going to build a greenhouse. Stone is got." This letter refers to one of the first greenhouses known to have been built in America.

Vegetable cultivation kept pace with the general progress in other branches of horticulture. Stephen Switzer, trained under the two great masters, London and Wise, stands out as one of the important people of the first half of the century, who was much concerned with the practical aspects of kitchen gardening. It was said of him that he was "a sound practical horticulturist, a man well versed in the botanical science of the day, in its most enlarged sense;

of considerable classical and literary attainments, and above all a religious character." Switzer did a prodigious amount of writing and left numerous works, most important of which is his *Ichnographia Rustica*. He tells that at the beginning of the century "every garden vegetable in a greater or less degree, was obtained from Holland. The supplyers of the Royal Family sent thither for Fruits and Pot Herbs; and the seedsmen obtained from thence their seeds." But after the first twenty-five years had passed, the situation improved tremendously. Cucumbers, which formerly were not seen on English tables until the close of May, were then ready by the first of March, and "the season of Pease and Beans was extended to a period from April to December, which previously only lasted two or three months."

When Peter Kalm, the Swedish naturalist for whom the mountain laurel, *Kalmia latifolia,* is named, stopped off in England on a trip he was making to America, he was so impressed by the vegetable gardens that he wrote: "most of them were at this time (February) covered with glass frames, which could be taken off at will . . . Russian matting over these, and straw over that four inches thick. These contained cauliflowers some four inches high. In the rest of the field were 'bell-glasses,' under which also cauliflower plants were set 3 or 4 under each bell-glass. Besides the afore-named beds, there were here long asparagus-beds. Their height above the ground was two feet; on the top they were similarly covered with glass, matting, and straw, which had just been all taken off at midday. The

Asparagus under them was one inch high and considerably thick."

This growing interest in the improvement of vegetable gardening was responsible for some valuable writing on the subject. One of the writers was John Abercrombie. Though born in Edinburgh, he spent most of his working years in and around London. He had wide experience and served as gardener to numerous noblemen and gentlemen of his day until 1770, when he developed an extensive business as a kitchen gardener, a forerunner of the present day truck gardener. Perhaps the fact that he had sixteen daughters was a reason for developing a big business. Abercrombie wrote *Every man his Own Gardener, Being a New and Much More Complete Gardener's Kalendar and General Director than Any One Hitherto Published*. Apparently no minute phase of practical gardening was untouched in this volume. It was published in twenty editions and for many years was a standard work on the subject. In order to be assured of some recognition Abercrombie paid to Thomas Mawe, a well known gardener to the Duke of Leeds, twenty pounds for the use of his name on the title page. In later editions the author's own name appeared on the title page with that of Mawe.

William Ellis and William Speechley were practical contributors to English horticulture. The former, a man widely traveled on the Continent, as well as in his own country, wrote in 1738 *The Timber Tree Improved, or The Best Practical Methods of Improving Different Lands with Proper Timber*. Four years later he published *Com-

FLORALIA *Some Paths and By-Paths*

plete *Modern Husbandry, Containing the Practice of Farming, Improvements on Fruit and Timber Trees.* The latter was not a scientist, but being a man of acute observation and long experience, he perhaps surpassed every practical gardener of his age. It is certain that he contributed more than anyone else to the improvement of the cultivation of the pineapple and vine; before the appearance of his two works there was little on record that afforded any material information regarding their cultivation. He wrote *A Treatise on the cultivation of the Vine* and also *A Treatise on the cultivation of the Pine Apple, and the management of the Hot-house; together with a description of every species of Insect that infect Hot-houses with effectual methods of destroying them.* This last seems an impossible claim. The pineapple seems to have been the subject of much discussion and experimentation and was successfully cultivated in England as a stove plant in 1723, though the first pineapple grown in England was given to Charles II by the gardener Rose. In 1716 Lady Mary Wortley Montagu spoke of having eaten pineapples at the table of the Elector of Hanover; she said she had never seen them before which, "as her Ladyshipe moved in the highest English Circles, she must, had they been introduced to Table here."

The path of scientific knowledge of plant cultivation expanded and the number of plants steadily increased. From foreign lands, especially from America, came frequent importations in infinite variety into European countries. And England, while maintaining her position as the promoter in garden thought, at the same time took place as leader in the acclimatization of these foreign visitors.

The gardens of England were greatly indebted to Peter Collinson (1693-1768), a distinguished naturalist, for the introduction of many new species of plants which he acquired from foreign countries and especially from the new world. Collinson carried on a correspondence over a long period with Linnaeus and the latter expressed his admiration for the man by naming *Collinsonia canadensis* after him. He was interested not only in natural history but in every other branch of science and was in constant communication with Franklin concerning electricity. The friendship, however, which benefited the garden world in a material way was that of Collinson and John Bartram, the great American naturalist, who lived on the Schuylkill River in Pennsylvania. Their correspondence, begun in 1734, was carried on for a generation and the letters of these men are a thrilling record of adventures, discoveries, experiments and exchanges in the plant world.

Peter Collinson was commemorated by Doctor Fothergill, and in the course of his writing he said: "That eminent naturalist, John Bartram, may almost be said to have been created such by my friend's [Peter Collinson's] assistance; he first recommended the collecting of seeds, and afterwards assisted in disposing of them in this country [England] and constantly excited him to persevere in investigating the plants of America, which he has executed with indefatigable labour through a long course of years, with amazing success."

FLORALIA *Some Paths and By-Paths*

Much of the plant material which found European homes came in from widely different sources. Some of these sources were missionaries in the cause of religion, explorers in the effort to enlighten the world and advance knowledge, and companies in the interest of commercial and territorial gain. Johnson in *English Gardening* says that previous to the century the number of "Exoticks" cultivated did not exceed 1,000 species, whereas during the period in question above 5,000 new ones were introduced.

The Botanic Garden of Chelsea was founded in 1673, though it was not actually established until 1686. It became effective, however, after 1721 when Sir Hans Sloane gave it permanency by a munificent gift. Philip Miller became its curator and rendered distinguished service in this capacity. He was one of the twenty members of the Society of Gardeners formed just after the first quarter of the century. Since most of the men who made up the membership of this group were nursery gardeners, their discussions were probably not as profound as those of the more learned societies, but much information of practical importance was contributed by them in the publication *Catalogus Plantarum*, 1730.

In the year 1760 Kew Gardens was founded by Augusta, Dowager Princess of Wales, mother of George III. This has since become one of the most famous and influential botanical institutions in the world. Much of the successful development of Kew Gardens in its early stage was due to Lord Bute, a leading horticulturist of the time, and to

FLORALIA *Some Paths and By-Paths*

William Aiton, the botanical superintendent. The latter left for his successors some remarkable records in *Hortus Kewensis*, a source of considerable information about the native, as well as the foreign plants grown under his supervision. George III, who was known as the Farmer King, shared his mother's enthusiasm for Kew. During her life, he willingly assisted her in cultivating and extending the ground, and after her death, he devoted much energy in directing the improvement of the gardens. Sir Joseph Banks, who was one of the King's intimates, became Chief Counsellor at Kew and by co-operating with the famous nurserymen there, aimed to make Kew a garden where every known plant, ornamental, as well as useful, could be found. The establishment of the Cambridge Botanical Garden followed that of Kew Gardens by a few years. This institution was founded by Dr. Walker, Vice-Master of Trinity College in 1763. According to a writer of the period: "He gave the scite comprising nearly five Acres, in trust to the Chancellor, Masters, and scholars of the University for the purpose of establishing the Garden. Thomas Martyn, the titular Professor of Botany, was appointed reader on Plants, and Charles, son of the celebrated Philip Miller (who had aided Dr. Walker in selecting the ground) was made first Curator."

The introduction and acclimatization of American plants influenced European gardens, and European gardens in turn influenced those of the new world. The earliest colonists brought seed and slips with them from their home gardens; some of these perished, and others throve alongside of native plants already growing in America. The strongest influence, as a whole, upon American gardens, however, was decidedly English; this was in order, since a majority of the colonists were English, although some of the more pretentious gardens of the eighteenth century were somewhat influenced by those of France. The natural style of landscape gardening which swept England during this period did not find a place in America until the following century.

The Royal Society, which had been formed in 1663 for the purpose of cultivating every department of science, furthered the formation of separate societies to keep pace with the rapid developments since the labors of one society were inadequate. The promotion of zoology and botany were the chief object of the Linnean Society, which was established in the year 1778 by Sir James Smith and named in honor of the great Swedish naturalist. In the botanical department of the museum of the Society there was a very rich collection containing the herbaria of Linnaeus, Smith, Pulteney, Relhan, Woodward, and Winch. The library had a particularly excellent collection of botanical works.

Because of the necessary leisure and inclination, gardening in the eighteenth century played a large part in the everyday affairs of the people and served as a medium for artistic expression. Just as the cultivated man had made the grand tour, so he now made gardens. Curiously enough, the garden world reflected as a mirror the social and political changes of a rapidly advancing age. The desire for freedom from restraint, the theme of the social order,

FLORALIA *Some Paths and By-Paths*

found willing apostles in the realm of horticulture, who in person, as well as in thought, invaded the classical school of garden design, tore down walls, and established a new order characterized by a naturalness directly opposed to the old order restrained by formalities. The foremost promoters of the new regime were English and so it was that England's influence in garden thought and practice crossed the channel and established its sway on the Continent.

CHAPTER II

The Rise of English Landscape Gardening

IN THE GARDEN WORLD it is significant that the year which marked the birth of the eighteenth century also marked the death of a great French garden designer, André le Nôtre. During the eighty-seven years of his life he had developed some beautiful formal gardens and had remodeled others that were the glory of France during the seventeenth century. With an artist for a creator and a king for a patron, classicism in garden design had reached its culmination at that time. Le Nôtre's lovely creations surpassed the fame of Italian gardens; and during his lifetime masters of the art came from Italy to learn of him and to admire his work. Under Louis XIV he had brought the formal garden to its zenith in the splendor of Versailles. As long as these gardens preserved their magnificence and as long as followers of the great designer lived and worked out the principles which he had laid down, France maintained her position as queen of this art, and gardens of every European country continued to feel the influence of French artificiality for many decades. But with the turn of the century and the passing of the spirit of Le Nôtre, shadows appeared which foretold a decline from formal garden architecture. Du Fresnoy, who succeeded Le Nôtre in 1700 as director of the French king's gardens, attempted to introduce the element of natural beauty but his example was not followed. And England, as she superseded France as first among the nations in many respects, moulded a style of her own in landscape gardening and emerged as a leader.

Just as any movement can be interpreted by a study of the people on whose shoulders it is carried forward, so the Naturalistic School may be understood by knowing something of the personalities and the publications of the men responsible for it. One of the early exponents of this school was John Locke, the English philosopher, who was born in the first half of the seventeenth century. His name belongs on the list of authors on horticulture. After having received the best education that his country could afford, he visited France and while staying at Montpelier paid much attention to the cultivation of the vine and the rearing of silk worms. Later there was printed from his original manuscript his observations upon the growth and culture of vines and olives, the production of silk, and the preservation of fruits.

The forerunners of this new school can be found among the poets of England who, since the second half of the seventeenth century, had been singing songs extolling untouched nature, and they, along with the leaders of the movement, Addison, Pope, Bridgeman, and Kent, can be called the pioneers of the new school. In fact, this revo-

FLORALIA *English Landscape Gardening*

lutionary movement extended beyond the interest of horticulturists and gardeners and was reflected in every method of expression. As never before, gardening served as a medium for the study of the nature of art. In this connection Pope said: "I believe it is no wrong observation, that persons of genius, and those who are most capable of art, are always most fond of nature; as such are chiefly sensible, that all art consists in the imitation and study of nature."

Addison's essay "Description of a Garden in the Natural Style" in *The Spectator* of June 25, 1712, sets forth the first criticism and suggestion in which an imitation of nature was advocated as a basis of gardening. He said: "Our British gardeners instead of humouring Nature, love to deviate from it as much as possible. Our Trees rise in Cones, Globes and Pyramids. We see the marks of the scissars upon every Plant and Bush. I do not know whether I am singular in my Opinion, but for my own part, I would rather look upon a tree in all its luxuriancy and Diffusion of Boughs and Branches, than when it is thus cut and trimmed into a Mathematical Figure; and cannot but fancy that an Orchard in Flower looks infinitely more delightful than all the little Labyrinths of the most finished Parterre." Pope followed Addison in decrying topiary work. "We seem," he said in *The Guardian* for September 29, 1713, "to make it our study to recede from nature, not only in the various tonsure of greens into the most regular and formal shapes, but even in monstrous attempts beyond the reach of art itself. We run into sculpture, and are yet better pleased to have our trees in the most aukward figures of men and animals, than in the most regular of their own." He went on to describe a possible catalogue which might have been issued by an enthusiast: "Adam and Eve in yew; Adam a little shattered by the fall of the tree of knowledge in the great storm; Eve and the Serpent, very flourishing. . . .

"St. George in box; his arm scarce long enough, but will be in condition to stick the dragon by next April.

"A green dragon of the same, with the tail of ground-ivy for the present.

"N. B. These two not to be sold separately. . . .

"Divers eminent modern poets in bays, somewhat blighted, to be disposed of, a pennyworth.

"A quick-set hog shot up into a porcupine, by its being forgot a week in rainy weather. . . ."

The first person to lay down precise rules for landscape gardening was Pope, though he acquired his information most likely from Bridgeman, the garden designer, whose importance in the development of the picturesque style is discussed below. Pope's "Epistle to Richard Boyle, Earl of Burlington" carried the twenty-four lines:

> To build, to plant, whatever you intend,
> To rear the column, or the arch to bend,
> To swell the terrace, or to sink the grot;
> In all, let nature never be forgot.
> But treat the Goddess like a modest fair,
> Nor over-dress, nor leave her wholly bare;

AN EIGHTEENTH-CENTURY GARDEN, FRONTISPIECE OF
THE CATALOGUS PLANTARUM

FLORALIA *English Landscape Gardening*

Let not each beauty ev'ry where be spy'd,
Where half the skill is decently to hide.
He gains all points, who pleasingly confounds,
Surprises, varies, and conceals the bounds.

Consult the genius of the place in all;
That tells the waters or to rise, or fall;
Or helps th' ambitious hill the heav'ns to scale,
Or scoops in circling theatres the vale;
Calls in the country, catches op'ning glades,
Joins willing woods, and varies shades from shades;
Now breaks, or now directs th' intending lines;
Paints as you plant, and, as you work, designs.

Still follow Sense, of ev'ry art the soul,
Parts ans'ring parts shall slide into a whole,
Spontaneous beauties all around advance,
Start ev'n from difficulty, strike from chance;
Nature shall join you; time shall make it grow,
A work to wonder at—perhaps a STOW.

Johnson in his *English Gardening* comments as follows: "The rules, from the shortness of the composition, are, of course, compendious, but they contain the fundamental principles of their art."

Addison at Bilton in Warwickshire and Pope at Twickenham established country places and though there was much planning and planting, by some strange contrariety neither place was made to assume the natural style which both men advocated so assiduously. Pope, who had ridiculed so many artificialities of formalism, showed his chief

FLORALIA *English Landscape Gardening*

inconsistency in his great pride in his grotto: "I have put my last hand to my works of this kind, in happily finishing the subterraneous way and grotto. I there found a spring of the clearest water, which falls in a perpetual rill, that echoes through the cavern day and night. From the river Thames you see through my arch up a walk of the wilderness to a kind of open temple, wholly composed of shells in the rustic manner; and from that distance under the temple, you look down through a sloping arcade of trees, and see the sails on the river passing suddenly and vanishing as through a perspective glass. When you shut the doors of this grotto it becomes on the instant, from a luminous room, a *camera obscura,* on the walls of which all the objects of the river, hills, woods, and boats are forming a moving picture in their visible radiations; and when you have a mind to light it up, it affords you a very different scene. It is finished with shells interspersed with pieces of looking-glass in angular forms; and in the ceiling is a star of the same material, at which, when a lamp of an orbicular figure of thin alabaster is hung in the middle, a thousand different rays glitter and are reflected over the place...." Perhaps it was the vapors of the grot and not damp weather which caused him to write to a friend: "I thank God for every wet day and for every fog, that gives me a headache, but prospers my work."

Stephen Switzer, who, besides his interest in kitchen gardens, was one of the first planters and designers of the landscape school, published in 1715 *The Nobleman, Gentleman and Gardener's Recreation.* "By which title,"

FLORALIA *English Landscape Gardening*

he said, "is meant the general Designing and Distributing of Country Seats into Gardens, Woods, Parks, Paddocks, etc: which I therefore call forest, or in more easie stile Rural Gardening." "This, Le Grand Manier," he says further, "is oppos'd to those crimping, diminutive and wretched performances we meet every day with... The top of these designs being in clipt plants, flowers, and other trifling decorations... fit only for little Town gardens, and not for the expensive Tracts of the Country."

While Addison and Pope wielded their pens in the promotion of the picturesque style, the garden designers, Bridgeman and Kent, were making practical contributions to it. Bridgeman came into notice about 1720. Although he left no volumes which expressed his ideas, Horace Walpole in his "Essay on Modern Gardening" a half century later comments on his method of work and attributes the victory of the then modern movement largely to Bridgeman's Ha-Ha, a new style of enclosure, a sunk fence or a trench in which a hedge was planted; it could not be seen until one was quite close to it. Although it served as a boundary between the garden and the rural expanse beyond, it was so inconspicuous a border line that the garden really merged into the open country. The breaking down of walls and enclosures which were such necessary parts of the formal French garden, and the bringing of the park into the garden were the most important steps in the transition between the classic and the landscape style. The name Ha-Ha has been popularly explained as an exclamation of surprise uttered when one suddenly came upon the sunken fence; students of the period conclude that this explanation is erroneous but unfortunately do not give what they believe to be the correct explanation. At any rate, the sunken wall was widely used and its influence made itself felt even across the ocean, for records show that in laying out the grounds of his Mount Vernon estate, Washington provided for a "Haw, Ha!" in two places.

Bridgeman was the first designer of the large and beautiful estate at Stowe and following him in this position was William Kent, born in 1685, who was to achieve fame for himself in the garden movement by making some entirely new departures. Kent frequently declared that he caught his taste in gardening from reading the picturesque descriptions of Spenser. Walpole said of him: "At that moment appeared Kent, painter enough to taste the charms of landscape, bold and opinionative enough to dare and to dictate, and born with a genius to strike out a great system from the twilight of imperfect essays. He leaped the fence, and saw that all Nature was a garden. He felt the delicious contrast of hill and valley changing imperceptibly into each other, tasted the beauty of the gentle swell, or concave scoop, and remarked how loose groves crowned an easy eminence with happy ornament, and while they called in the distant view between their graceful stems, removed and extended the perspective by elusive comparison."

The great principles on which Kent worked were perspective, light and shade. Where spaces were too wide open he filled in by introducing groups of trees and sometimes temples. He achieved wonderful effects in the management of water; a more or less straight stream was taught to meander or serpentine seemingly at its pleasure. His enthusiasm for his cause outran his judgment, and when he imitated nature even in her faults by planting dead trees in Kensington Gardens, he was criticised and laughed out of the "excess." His ruling principle seems to have been "Nature abhors a straight line."

The influences that were operating in England which fostered the cult of country life found a counterpart in France through the writings and teachings of the philosopher, Jean Jacques Rousseau, who early broke with the exaggerated formalism of a superficial civilization, and proclaimed romantic joys of rural pursuits and the virtue and beauty of a life close to nature.

The foremost exponent of picturesque gardening was the poet Shenstone (1714-1763) who wrote: "Art should never be allowed to set foot in the province of Nature," and yet like Kent and other advocates he swung so far from formalism that he used artifices to make nature appear more natural than it was. He suggested the following method of making an avenue seem what it was not: "An avenue that is widened in front and planted there with yew trees, then firs, then with trees more and more fady, till they end in the almond willow or silver osier; will produce a very remarkable deception."

He inherited his patriarchal estate, Leasowes, and in 1745 much against his will, went there to beautify his property and his efforts must have been successful for Whately said: "It is a perfect picture of his mind, simple, elegant and amiable . . ." By investing the greater part of his fortune in his place and ever mindful of "polite taste" and "refinement" he made it a most perfect example of the new style of gardening. His advice on matters pertaining to landscape gardening was much sought after. Dr. Johnson said of his work: "Now was excited his delight in rural pleasures, and his ambition of rural elegance: he began from this time to point his prospects, to diversify his surface, to entangle his walks, and to wind his waters; which he did with such judgment and such fancy as made his little domain the envy of the great and admiration of the skilful; a place to be visited by travellers, and copied by designers." However, his pride in his possession and his desire to further excel in the beautification of his property caused him to spend too much money and the closing years of his life were made unhappy from the constant annoyance of creditors. Although he had made of it a perfect paradise his biographer, Dr. Johnson, comments that, "His groves were haunted by beings very different from fauns and fairies." From "Unconnected Thoughts on Gardening," in a work published in three volumes soon after his death, can be obtained Shenstone's interpretation of the principles of the prevailing style which in brief were to present a scene at once varied and pleasing to the eye.

Following Shenstone's volumes by a few years came Thomas Whately's *Observations on Modern Gardening*. Loudon pronounced it the grand fundamental and stand-

FLORALIA *English Landscape Gardening*

ard work on English gardening. It treats first of the kind of materials the landscape gardener has to work with; secondly of the scenes producible with them; and lastly the subjects of gardening. He illustrates his points by giving descriptions of Blenheim, Claremont, Leasowes, and Stowe. Many volumes by other authors came out in rapid succession at this time, all advocating the imitation of nature, and they contributed very largely to the growth and success of the new school.

With the gradual development and crystallization of the new school the English people not only became aware of accomplishment, but also became conscious of a style all their own. Gray voiced this feeling when he wrote: "The only proof of our original talent in matter of pleasure is our skill in gardening and the laying-out of grounds. And this is no small honour to us, since neither Italy nor France, has ever had the least notion of it, nor yet do the least comprehend it when they see it. It is very certain, we copied nothing from them, nor had anything but nature for our model. [It is not forty years since] the art was born among us; and it is sure that there was nothing in Europe like it, and as sure, we then had no information on this head from China at all."

This reference to China was occasioned by the fact that at this time Sir William Chambers, who belonged to the prevailing school, advocated Chinese methods of erecting buildings which would produce various emotions. The pagoda at Kew and other temples were designed by him and are monuments to a lasting fashion promoted by Sir

FLORALIA *English Landscape Gardening*

William because of the influence of such structures upon him when he traveled in China. The practice of the naturalistic style had been carried on in that country for more than two thousand years. In his *Dissertation on Oriental Gardening,* Chambers said: "The Chinese Gardeners take nature for their pattern and their aim is to imitate all her beautiful irregularities... yet they are not so attached to her as to exclude all appearance of art. Art must supply the scantiness of nature and not only be employed to produce variety but also novelty and effect: for the simple arrangements of nature are to be met with in every common field to a certain degree of perfection, and are therefore too familiar to excite any strong sensations in the mind of the beholder or to produce any uncommon degree of pleasure." Ornamental details of English garden art, as well as furniture, porcelain, and wall paper, felt the effect of China's example, but the fundamentals were not affected by this foreign influence.

The name of Lancelot Brown or "Capability Brown," so called because he could always see great capabilities in a piece of ground about which he was consulted, stands out in the landscape garden world of the middle of the century. He designed and executed estates for many of the prominent and fashionable people of his day, though the work of Brown could not approach that of Kent. He was more successful in the treatment of water than in the treatment of the woodland. Apparently his capacity for ideas was not as great as his capacity for inducing the country squires to have their estates altered. His plans and designs were more or less the same and were easily copied; unfortunately innumerable inferior imitations resulted.

This garden designer or landscape gardener, a new term which was introduced by Shenstone, did not confine his activities to creating, but destroyed with avidity many beautiful gardens that belonged to other days. Because of his destructions he was assailed by many prominent in garden circles. The spade and axe were at work in every estate, and so rapidly did the face of the country alter that in 1772 Sir William Chambers declared that if the mania were not checked, in a few years more, three trees would not be found in a straight line from the Land's End to the Tweed. Sir Uvedale Price in his *Essay on the Picturesque* (1794) says: "At a gentleman's place in Cheshire, there is an avenue of oaks. Mr. Brown absolutely condemned it, but it now stands a noble monument of the triumph of the natural feelings of the owner over the narrow and systematic ideas of a professed improver. One is thankful that a few people had strength of mind enough to resist the all-powerful Brown."

Since the days of Queen Anne the "pretty gardens" had been ridiculed, and although the process of copying nature advanced very swiftly it was not until the middle years of the century in which Brown was active that destruction was so widespread. Fortunately many plates and prints exist at the present time which give an adequate idea of the lay-out and plans of the seventeenth century gardens. Mrs. Cecil Rockley in her history of English gardening says that if authors had foreseen the annihilation that was to befall so many gardens, they could hardly have more carefully preserved their designs. These can be seen in Plot's *Staffordshire,* Atkyns's *Gloucester, Britannia Illustrata,* 1709, with a series of views by Kip, and in other works published early in the eighteenth century.

The inevitable outcome of many influences fighting for predominance in English landscape gardening during the eighteenth century was a clash. Disagreements came about over the way in which these imitations of nature should be directed. The introduction of the Chinese style and Brown's destructions were two of the factors underlying the disagreements. Mr. Sidding summed up the situation by saying that "formality gone mad was supplanted by informality gone equally mad." The leaders of the cause had very decided views and toward the latter part of the century quarrels broke out. Walpole and Mason stood together and Chambers represented the opposite side.

Humphrey Repton, who was an admirer of Brown, as well as of Le Nôtre, took part in these discussions, and during the last years of the century he was an influential character in the English garden group. He said he did not profess to follow either of the men whose work he admired, but he endeavored to adopt some of the grandeur of Le Nôtre and enough of the grace of Brown to produce charm in the natural landscape. He was a very diligent and scientific student and rather an exception in that he did not always alter what he found. He gave unwearied effort to make his improvements suit a particular place. A "red book" was created for each place which he designed, in which was given first a picture of the place as he found it and then another picture as he proposed the place to look after he had finished his improvements. When *Observations on the Theory and Practice of Landscape Gardening* was published in 1797, there were flaps on the illustrations which enabled one to get before and after versions of the gardens as he planned them. Repton, who was spoken of as an improver of English taste, was apparently the last of the designers of the period in which the upheaval of the garden world had taken place.

William Gilpin, prebendary of Salisbury and vicar of Boldre in New Forest, near Lynington, did some writing on the "Picturesque" during the last decade of the century, in which he advocated some very excellent principles of garden design. His travel books, published between 1783 and 1809, and his *Three Essays* which appeared in 1792, show him to have been a person of much originality and wisdom. He suggests that the designs to imitate are those which are pleasing whether they be natural or acquired. To do this, taste in the imitator is the chief requisite. Gilpin very justly remarks that the comparative virtue of taste and expense is remarkable; the former with very little of the latter will always produce something pleasing, while the utmost efforts of the latter unaided by the former are ineffectual. All his observations are illustrated by examples. He draws on much of his native English scenery for the purpose and describes the following estates for a similar purpose, Blenheim, Burleigh, and Castlehill. His writing, done in a delightful style, and very generally read at that

FLORALIA *English Landscape Gardening*

time, served most effectively in forming the national taste.

Sir Uvedale Price advocated for those interested in landscape a study of the principles of painting "not to the exclusion of nature, but as an assistant in the study of her works." Beautiful effects could be secured first by boldness, abruptness, depth, and sudden contrasts of shade, and second by gentle undulations, with soft blendings of light and shade.

Just as France had wielded her influence in the classic style of a preceding century, so the English gardens with their "taste and refinement" were now popular and fashionable. Most of the countries on the Continent were affected by this mode. At the Imperial Park of Tsar Koe-Selo, a garden was created in the English style. In Austria, as well as in Germany, appeared some lovely reflections of this prevailing fashion. The garden of Petit Trianon, built in 1759 as a haven of peace and quiet, was at first formal but later in the century under the influence of Marie Antoinette, it became the first example of the English garden in France. In the hundred years that intervened between the passing of the great Le Nôtre and the school which he represented, and the dawn of the nineteenth century, landscape gardening had become the established practice of England.

CHAPTER III

A Company of English Gardeners

THE PIONEERS of the new style of gardening discouraged the inclusion of the flower garden as part of the landscape. Flowers were relegated to the background, often finding homes in kitchen gardens where, although there was a mania for tearing down enclosures, high brick walls served as a protection for the regularly laid out beds in which vegetables and blossoms throve side by side. But even when the proponents of landscape gardening had reached their top-most peaks of enthusiasm, and gardens were being merged into parks, there were many excellent gardeners who carried on the work of floriculture in a quiet way. Many people felt that a garden, no matter how it was laid out, was not a garden unless there were flowers in it. It was due largely to the Society of Gardeners which was formed early in the century that horticulture in its more practical aspects made such tremendous advances. The society was made up of the following:

Thomas Fairchild   John Alston
Robert Furber   Obadiah Low

FLORALIA *A Company of English Gardeners*

Philip Miller	William Hood
John Thompson	Richard Cole
Christopher Gray	William Welstead
Francis Hunt	Benjamin Whitmill
Samuel Driver	Samuel Hunt
Moses James	John James
George Singleton	Stephen Bacon
Thomas Bickerstaff	William Spencer

These men, who lived in or around London, for the most part were nursery owners. For six years the society held monthly meetings in Newhall's Coffee-house in Chelsea. The members were required to bring to the meetings specimens of the plants which they were growing in their respective gardens. There was a general discussion of the plant material, its nature and possibilities, by the assembled group. The plants were registered and names and descriptions recorded, and these records were kept with the idea of publishing them, for the society felt that the public would benefit from such a work inasmuch as the nomenclature of plants at the time was very vague. In less than a decade after the society had been organized there appeared *Catalogus Plantarum, A Catalogue of Trees, Shrubs, Plants and Flowers Both Exotic and Domestic Which are propagated for Sale in the Gardens Near London Divided, according to their different Degrees of Hardiness, into particular Books, or Parts: in each of which the Plants are Ranged in Alphabetical Order. To which are added The Characters of the Genus, and an Enumera-*

FLORALIA *A Company of English Gardeners*

tion of all the particular Species which are at present to be found in the several nurseries near London, with directions for the proper Soil and Situation, in which Each particular Kind is found to Thrive. By a Society of Gardeners London, Printed in the Year 1730. The work was dedicated as follows: "To the Right Honourable Thomas Earl of Pembroke and Montgomery." After eulogizing the Earl for being a patron of whatever intends to improve useful knowledge, the dedication closes with: "We know your Lordship to be more judicious, than to expect polite language from us, whose Conversation is mostly with Speechless Vegetables. . . Permit us to subscribe ourselves Your Lordship's Most Humble and Devoted Servants the Society of Gardeners."

The preface sheds much light on the horticultural situation in the early part of the century. It opens with the following paragraph: "Providence having allotted to us a Situation in a temperate Climate, as remote from the scorching Rays of the Sun of the Torrid, as from the piercing Colds and nipping Frosts of the Frozen Zone; by Reasons of which our Soil and Atmosphere are adapted to the Culture and Nurture of most plants in the Universe, whether from Warmer or Colder Climates either useful for the various Purposes of Life, or delightful by their Beauty and Variety; it would be a Neglect scarce pardonable, to suffer So valuable a Blessing to pass unregarded and unimproved." However, the society seemed pleased over the advantage of the time in which they were working. They felt that due to the cessation of wars, to wise rulers, and to the Royal Society, which had been established for the improvement of natural knowledge, as well as to generous patrons, the "Business of Gardening is daily reduced to a much Greater Certainty."

The publication of *Catalogus Plantarum* was a natural outgrowth of the work of the society. At first they employed an eminent artist to make drawings and paintings of fruits and flowers and plants which they discussed at their meetings and in this way they acquired a very valuable collection of drawings. Soon after, they felt that it would be well to publish the observations that they had "minuted" down from time to time. The original plan was to publish the observations in a catalogue of several parts, one of trees and shrubs, one of the "Exoticks," which were preserved in stoves, and another of various flowers for the pleasure garden. For each section there were to be plates of some of the new and curious varieties included therein. However, the undertaking was evidently too big a one for men who were regularly employed, since no part of the records was published after Part I, on trees and shrubs, appeared.

In it more than one hundred and fifty trees and shrubs are recorded. The descriptions are accurately done. The method was "to place the most generally received Latin name of each Tree and Shrub, by which it is called amongst the Modern Botanists, and then have added one or more Synonyms, from the most noted of the antient writers in Botany; to which is subjoined the Common English Name in small Capitals, that it may appear at the first view, to

Title-Page of the Catalogus Plantarum

such Persons who have not been acquainted with the Latin name." The description of the *Acacia* is an interesting example:

Acacia; The Binding Bean Tree, or Ægyptian-Thorn.
The Characters are:

It hath ramose (or branching) Leaves. The Flowers (which consist of one Leaf, and are tubulous, producing several Stamina, or Threads, out of each) closely adhere together, forming a little round Globe. The Seed are contained in hard Pods, and are separated from each other by transverse Diaphragms, being closely surrounded with a sweetish pulpy substance.

The Species are:
1. Acacia; Americana, Abruae foliis triacanthos... —Three-Thorn'd Acacia, or Locust Tree.
2. Acacia; Americana, Abruae foliis triacanthos; floribus coccineis—The Scarlet-Flowering Acacia: vulgô.
3. Acacia; Caroliniana, aquatica...—Water Acacia.

The first of these *Acacias* hath been an old inhabitant of *English* gardens. Several large Trees of it remaining in the Bishop of *London's* garden at *Fulham* and in the *Physic Garden* at *Chelsea* in the last of which places it hath produced Flowers, which are very small, and of a greenish color without Scent. The flowers drop off without producing any Pods with us. This tree is very hardy and of quick Growth, but is very subject to be broken by Winds; if planted in Places too much exposed thereto.

The Second and Third Sorts were raised from Seeds

FLORALIA *A Company of English Gardeners*

which were sent from *Carolina* by Mr. *Catesby, Anno.* 1723. They are both very hardy; but the *Water Acacia* is a quicker Grower.

Acacia of Virginia, vide Pseudoacacia.

At the back of the volume are twenty-one colored plates after Van Huysum; on some plates more than one kind of plant is illustrated.

Of this company of gardeners, certain ones stand out: Thomas Fairchild as a horticulturist, Robert Furber as a nurseryman, and Philip Miller as a botanist. Each left something worthy of note which lives on after more than two hundred years have passed.

Thomas Fairchild, from all indications, was a very intelligent man. Although most of his work was done before the horticultural world had felt the impact of Charles Linnaeus, his writings show him to have been a person of general information, as well as one who was fond of scientific research. In his garden at Hoxton he performed many experiments to demonstrate the sexuality of plants and to show that plants possessed a circulatory system. In the *Philosophical Transactions* for 1724, he published the result of other experiments under the title: *On the Different and Some Time Contrary Motion of the Sap in Plants.*

Fairchild's work brought him the admiration of his contemporaries. Richard Bradley was one of these, though he might have been prompted by a selfish motive for he frequently made use of Fairchild's experiments in his prolific writing. But whatever the motive was, Bradley frequently referred to Fairchild as one of the most skilled gardeners of the time. *The City Gardener: containing the most experienced method of cultivating and ordering such Evergreens, Fruit Trees, Flowering Shrubs, Flowers, Exotick Plants, &c. as will be ornamental and thrive best in the London Gardens* was Fairchild's most important publication. As the title indicates, the purpose of the work was to make known the plants that would grow around London since "Every thing will not prosper because of the smoke of the Sea Coal."

Fairchild died in 1729 and something of the nature of the man is understood by a provision made in his will for a sum of money which established "The Fairchild Lecture." He stipulated that annually on Whit-Tuesday a sermon should be delivered in St. Leonard's, Shoreditch, "On the wonderful works of God in the Creation; or on the Certainty of the resurrection of the dead, proved by the certain changes of the animal and vegetable parts of the creation." This lecture has been delivered during all the years that have passed. The Bishop of London annually appoints a rector who endeavors to carry out in his sermon the founder's purpose in the light of modern developments.

The name of Robert Furber follows that of Thomas Fairchild on the membership list of the most famous gardeners and nurserymen of the time. Furber was the founder of the nursery at Kensington and although little is known about the life and work of this man, enough remains to mark him a unique personality of the world in which he moved.

There are evidences of a comradely spirit and mutual understanding prevailing among the members of the Society of Gardeners. The *Catalogus Plantarum* is an example of co-operation and not competition, for it was a catalogue of trees for sale in their respective nurseries. Another instance is given; when Philip Miller's *Gardener's and Florist's Dictionary* appeared in 1724 there was appended to the second volume Furber's *Catalogue of Curious Trees and Plants*. The introductory notice is as follows: "For the satisfaction of such gentlemen that are curious in collecting of foreign trees and shrubs and are not willing to be at the expense of building Stoves and Greenhouses, I have here set down a catalogue of such trees and shrubs, both Exotick and Domestick, as will prosper in our Climate, in the open ground, as hath been several years experienced by Mr. Robert Furber, Gardener over against Hide Park Gate at Kensington, where any gentleman may be furnished with any of the following Trees and Shrubs at Reasonable Rates."

An edition of this catalogue of Furber's was published separately from Miller's *Dictionary*. The preface says: "The design of presenting this Catalogue is to inform the lovers of gardening of the names of several curious Exotick and Domestick plants that are hardy enough to stand abroad and flourish in our climate. I shall avoid mentioning their Names at length as they are inserted in the Botanical Authors, but content myself rather by calling them by such Names only as they are generally known in England."

Another contribution which made history in the garden world was the publication, in 1730, of a catalogue of nursery flowers by Furber, which was made up of twelve large prints, one for each month of the year. The first print is for January and in it are the flowers that bloom in that month. "We would have chosen to begin with the Spring months, viz., March, April and May, and have thrown the three following summer months to those which properly relate to autumn; and then took in those of the winter; but the Common Custom of beginning the year with January, will excuse us." No text accompanied the twelve months of flowers.

This catalogue was so well received by the public that in 1732 Furber published *The Flower Garden Display'd*. The title page is bordered with a wreath of twenty-four different kinds of blossoms, all duly numbered with their names listed below. He used the same plates as in the 1730 edition but they were reduced to a smaller size. The flowers are profusely and casually arranged in a handsome vase; a few, to add to the grace and informality of the picture, have tumbled to the table. Each flower in the plate is numbered and at the bottom the name of the flower is given according to its number. In giving his reasons for his catalogue, Furber says: "It will be a means of informing the Publick of the Great Variety of Flowers, in all their stations, at every season of the year. It may be thought, perhaps, that the winter months are void of

FLORALIA *A Company of English Gardeners*

the Delights expected in a Flower-Garden; but the mistake will soon be discovered by any curious observer, when he shall find, that there are at least two and thirty flowers of different kinds then in their splendour."

In the introduction he wrote: "It being an observation made by many persons (and we think with much reason) that to know only the names of flowers, and to be ignorant of their culture, might occasion a continual expense in procuring such Rarities, which one day, might live with them, and, for want of this necessary knowledge, might perish the next." There is a page giving a short explanation of the most difficult terms which are made use of in the book. One of the terms defined is: "Exposure, the Position of a wall or bank, with respect to the Sun: Thus, a warm exposure signifies where the Sun may come very much." Furber also remarked that the prints were very useful not only for the curious in gardening, but likewise for painters, carvers, Japaners, also for the ladies as patterns for working and painting in water colors.

The year 1732 was a full one for the nurseryman, for in addition to the above book, he also issued *Fruits for every month in the year, illustrated by twelve plates.* These were prints of the best kinds of fruits grown at that time.

A second edition of *The Flower Garden Display'd* was brought out in 1734 and in it Mr. Furber became more confident in giving advice in "the art of raising flowers to bloom without any trouble in full perfection in the depth of winter." To this was appended *A Flower Garden for Gentlemen and Ladies, or The Art of raising Flowers to*

FLORALIA *A Company of English Gardeners*

blow in the depth of winter; also the method of raising Salleting, Cucumbers &c. at any time of the year.

Furber's catalogues are delightful to look at, and they form a very valuable and complete record of the flowers which were grown in England at the time when they were published.

Philip Miller was, because of his ability and achievement, the most famous member of this group of men who combined their efforts to further good horticulture. A contemporary said that Miller was sent to the garden kingdom when he was needed most, and Johnson says that in him were combined the perfect botanist and horticulturist. These superlatives were an expression of gratitude for a man of practical judgment and skill, as well as one of much scientific knowledge. Miller was a pioneer in the introduction of the new plants that were coming into England from every country and every climate, and he also increased the number of plants that had previously been grown in this country. He said that "gardening never arrived to any considerable pitch in England until about thirty years last past."

Sir Hans Sloane made over the Botanic Garden in Chelsea in 1722 to the Worshipful Company of Apothecaries. He had for many years taken a lively interest in the garden and in 1684 wrote Ray an account of a visit paid to it. "I was the other day at Chelsea, and find that the artifices used by Mr. Watts have been very effectual for the Preservation of his plants, insomuch that this severe winter has scarce killed any of his fine plants. One thing I much

FLORALIA *A Company of English Gardeners*

wonder to see *Cedrus Montis Libani* ... should thrive so well, as without pot or green House, to be able to propagate itself by Layers this spring. Seeds grown last Autumn have as yet thriven very well." Sir Hans appointed Philip Miller as Curator and he fulfilled the duties of this position in a very distinguished manner over a long period of time. This generous act of philanthropy in establishing the garden permanently carried with it these conditions: that the Company should pay £5 per annum for it, and that the demonstrator of the Company, in its name, should deliver annually fifty new species of plants to the Royal Society, until the number amounted to 2,000. This presentation of plants commenced in 1722, and continued until 1773, at which time they had presented, 2,550 species.

During the years that Miller served as Curator of the Chelsea Garden he did some valuable writing. His works are important rather than numerous. His *Gardener's and Florist's Dictionary* dedicated to the Worshipful Company of Apothecaries, which made its first appearance in 1724, was the greatest horticultural work of the time. Thomas Martyn said that this edition was merely the germ of those which succeeded it. This new work was sponsored by many of the most famous of the contemporary gardeners and nurserymen. The "Catalogue of Ever Greens" in the 1724 edition is worthy of note. The number amounted only to twelve: Alaternus, Arbutus, Bay, Box, Holly, Juniper, Laurel, Laurustinus, Phillyrea, Pyracantha, Flalia, Green Privet (which is not properly an evergreen) and Yew. Mr. Miller prescribes the manner of laying out a pleasure garden; and gives directions for building a greenhouse or conservatory.

Seven years later, in 1731, Mr. Miller published his *Gardeners Dictionary* in folio. This is commonly regarded as the first edition and is entitled: *The Gardeners Dictionary: Containing the Methods of Cultivating and Improving the Kitchen, Fruit and Flower Garden. As also, the Physick Garden, Wilderness Conservatory, and Vineyard, According to the Practice of the Most Experienced Gardeners of the present age. Interspersed with the History of the Plants, the Character of Each Genus, and the names of all the particular Species in Latin and English.* It was printed in London for the author by C. Rivington at the Bible and Crown in St. Paul's Church-yard, and was illustrated with copper plates. The frontispiece is an old-fashioned garden and plantation with a council of heathen divinities superintending the greenhouse, stove and wine press. The *Dictionary* was inscribed to Sir Hans Sloane, President, the Council and Fellows of the Royal Society.

The second edition, published in 1733, varied little from the first, nor did the others until the sixth which was published in 1752. This was the first complete edition of the *Dictionary*. The seventh edition in 1759 was even more complete and in it was adopted the classical system of Linnaeus. Miller had been trained in the schools of Tournefort and of Ray, and since he was well versed in their methods, it was not without reluctance and much persuasion that he embraced the Linnaean system. This was the final blow to the line which divided the gardener and the botanist. The eighth and last edition was published in 1768. "This is allowed by his friends and even his enemies to be a work of extraordinary merit."

In 1755 Miller began to publish in folio numbers his "Figures of Plants" which had been made for the *Gardeners Dictionary*. There were three hundred colored plates and these with the descriptive texts which accompany them make the two folio volumes completed in 1760. These plates contained more botanical dissections than any other work that had appeared in England up to that time.

The author apologizes for the many editions of his work, but tells of the necessity of it because of the very great improvements that had been made in the art of gardening since the first edition was published; the number of plants cultivated in England being more than double those which were known in 1731. John Rogers in speaking of it a hundred years later said: "This valuable publication may be regarded, indeed, as the first bright beam of gardening issuing from the dark cloud of ignorance in which it had previously been enveloped. It may be almost said to have laid the foundation of all the horticultural taste and knowledge in Europe." Linnaeus justly remarked that Miller's was a botanical as well as a horticultural dictionary. Thomas Martyn who edited an edition of this work after the author's death said: "There have been few books treating of any Art or Science, which have maintained their ground in manner unrivalled so long as Mr. Miller's *Gardener's Dictionary*, near half a century having elapsed between the publication of the first edition in octavo, and the last in quarto."

The Gardener's Kalendar, Directing what Works are necessary to be done every month in the Kitchen, Fruit and Pleasure Gardens was published by Miller early in his career. This work was apparently influenced by the writings of John Evelyn. Mr. Miller justifies himself in writing this volume by saying: "In view of having written the *Gardener's Dictionary* the present performance may perhaps be judged superfluous; the *Kalendar* is portable on all occasions either in the Closet or Garden." In a later edition of this, one published in 1761, was included "A Short Introduction to a Knowledge of the Science of Botany."

Miller, who was a Fellow in the Royal Society, read many papers at their meetings. One of his earliest recorded is "A Method of Raising Some Exotick Seeds." And another especially interesting at this time is "An Account of Some Experiments Relating to the Flowering of Tulips, Narcissus, etc. in Winter by Placing Their Bulbs upon Glasses of Water." This now popular method of causing bulbous plants to flower was advocated by Furber in the 1734 edition of *The Flower Garden Display'd.*

Philip Miller was born near London and most of his life was spent in and around that city. He possessed extraordinary talents which peculiarly fitted him for the work he carried on for so many years. A contemporary testified that "Amidst an ungenial soil and a forbidding climate, he had successfully produced the rarest and most beautiful exotics, and afforded to his countrymen the gratification of beholding the finest specimens of vegetation which a tropical climate can produce, without their being themselves exposed to its scorching and oppressing influence. Thus has he, by the aid of science, changed, as it were, the very climate of his country, so far as his plants were concerned; and, by an intimate examination into the principles of vegetation, he has converted the most simple elements of nature into the most beautiful specimens of horticulture." Miller was, no doubt, influenced by the great personalities of the botanical world with whom he associated. Sir Hans Sloane was long one of his patrons, and later in life he became a correspondent not only of the great Linnaeus but of many of the most eminent botanists on the Continent. He was closely associated also with the leading nurserymen and florists of his own country. Dr. Pultney says Miller raised himself to a degree of eminence rarely, if ever before, equaled in the character of a gardener. The eminence was thoroughly deserved, for not only was he a highly skilled horticulturist, but a good botanist as well.

CHAPTER IV

Noble Patrons of the Gentle Art

"*The innocent Delights to be enjoyed in a well dispos'd and artfully managed Fruit, Kitchen and Pleasure-Garden have allured many learned and curious persons, nobility and gentry, to encourage this profitable and delightful art, and these have not contented themselves with the narrow Compass, and mean stock of our former poorly-furnished Gardens, but they have industriously procured from abroad, Trees, Plants, Flowers, and Fruits not only from our own Plantation in America, but those also of other parts of Europe, nay, even Asia and Africa.*"—Preface, Catalogus Plantarum.

THROUGHOUT THE EIGHTEENTH CENTURY numerous wealthy men devoted their time and talents to the promotion of horticulture. Some of these patrons were especially active early in the century, and that the efforts of this group were appreciated and served as inspiration is shown by the following paragraph from the *Catalogus Plantarum*: "These generous encouragers have inspired these ingenious gardeners to make the study of vegetation their business, and to improve the cultivation not only of trees, plants and flowers of our own growth, but also to procure and naturalize foreign ones of many different climates to our own; and they have by great Pains, Industry, and artful Management, happily succeeded in many Things, not only to their own satisfaction, but also to that of their Employees; May we hope without Arrogancy ... to be able not only to vie with, but to out-do most of the same profession in Europe."

The Sherard brothers, William (1659-1728) and James (1666-1737) had done much to foster good gardening and plant importation before the century dawned. Dr. William Sherard was one of the most munificent patrons and cultivators of exotic botany that appeared during this Golden Age. While he served as British Consul at Sedekio near Smyrna he cultivated a beautiful garden, and, according to Johnson in *English Gardening*, "he collected the most extensive herbarium that was ever formed by the exertions of one individual." It contained 12,000 species. At the same time his brother James built up at Eltham in Kent, a very extensive garden in which grew many rare plants. Consul William Sherard founded a botanical professorship at Oxford and appointed John James Dillenius as first professor, "which place he held, filling its duties, with respect to the garden at least, very assiduously, till he died there April 1747." Sir Arthur Rawdon was influenced by the Sherards, and sent collectors to foreign countries to gather plants for his magnificent garden at Moira in Ireland.

FLORALIA *Patrons of the Gentle Art*

In addition to the Sherards, there were many other early "Procurers of Plants and Encouragers of Gardening," some of whom were especially noteworthy because of their generosities. Among the latter were Dr. Compton, late Bishop of London, whose garden was at Fulham; The Duke of Argyle; Sir John Hill, then only Dr. Hill; Dr. Pitcairn (for whom Pitcairn Island was named); Dr. Fothergill; and the Dukes of Marlborough and of Cumberland. One of the early correspondents with travelers abroad was Dr. Uvedale of Enfield who built up a fine collection which he later sold to Sir Robert Walpole. Among the women who served as patronesses were the Duchess of Portland, and Her Grace the Duchess of Beaufort, who brought together in her gardens at Badminton a remarkable collection of rare plants. Another royal patron who must not be overlooked was the Earl of Pembroke. His gardens at Wilton were noteworthy because of their extent and beauty and large collection of "Exoticks."

Towering head and shoulders over his contemporaries, not only as patron and as botanist, but also as an individual of unique parts, was the ardent collector, Sir Hans Sloane. The following informal estimate pictures something of the man in several aspects: "I am but just come from Sir Hans Sloane's where I have beheld many odder things than himself, though none so inconsistent; however I will not rail for he has given me some of his trumpery to add to my collection, and till I get a better they shall remain there." So wrote the Duchess of Portland, herself an encourager of the gentle art of gardening, to her dear friend Mrs. Elizabeth Montagu. However odd and inconsistent the gentleman in question was, and those characteristics are granted without dispute, posterity can never complain, for in his remarkable collection that noble institution, the British Museum, had its birth, and Sir Hans will be remembered through the ages as its founder.

Born in 1660 of Scottish parents in County Down, Ireland, he came to England at the age of twenty to study medicine at the Apothecaries' Hall in London. From his youth up, Hans had been a devoted student of natural history and in him is an interesting example of the combined botanist and physician. Adjacent to the Apothecaries' Hall was the Chelsea Garden and here Hans Sloane had daily association with John Ray, the father of natural history in England, and also made the acquaintance of Robert Boyle, who is known for his work on gases. Young Hans found stimulation in acquaintanceships with these outstanding scientists just as at a later time Linnaeus was moved to do better work by early meetings with leading scientists of his own country.

Following the custom of going to the Continent in order to take a degree, Sloane spent several years in Paris and from available accounts he was a conscientious worker. "Upon his arrival in Paris he attended the Hospital of La Charité and the lectures of the chief professors of Botany, Chemistry, and Anatomy in that City, which afforded him full employment for the day. He entered at six in the morning the Royal Garden of Plants with Monsieur Tour-

Sir Hans Sloane

nefort, who demonstrated the plants after the order of Gaspar Bauhin in his *Pinax,* till eight, then Monsieur Duforty explained their virtues till ten; and at two in the afternoon Monsieur du Verney read upon Anatomy till four, and was succeeded by Monsieur Parlyon, the chemical professor, who discoursed in French on the operations to be performed that day by Monsieur Favens. Mr. Sloane was assiduous in his attendance on all these Professors."

As a result of such strenuous study, he "maintained a thesis with great applause" and was granted a degree of Doctor of Physic. In 1684 he returned to London, bringing with him the collection of rare specimens that he had made in France. Recognition came rapidly to the young man; he was made a Fellow of the Royal Society in 1685 and two years later a Fellow in the Royal College of Physicians. In addition to these honors Sloane was recommended by the famous physician, Thomas Sydenham, to his patients since Sydenham, hampered by gout, could no longer attend them.

Before the young doctor could begin his practice he received an invitation from the newly appointed governor of Jamaica to accompany him as physician to that island country. So glorious an opportunity to study the flora and fauna of the West Indies could not be passed by, and in due course, in December, 1687, the party landed in Jamaica. Sloane collected from the beginning of his stay and this was fortunate for the Governor died after he had been there only fifteen months, and his widow requested the young doctor to accompany her to England. He had gathered 800 species of plants which he planned to carry home, in addition to a lizard, a crocodile and a long yellow snake. The plants were carried safely, but such good fortune did not attend the rest of the cargo. The crocodile, not taking to the cramped quarters of a tub of salt water, expired, the lizard jumped overboard, and the snake, not finding an earthen jar commodious enough, pushed off the wooden cover and crawled to the top of the deck house. Sloane was delighted with the snake's new home since the numerous rats in the rafters of the deck house furnished food for it. There were others, unfortunately, of a contrary opinion, for he records that the "footmen and other domestics of Her Grace who, being afraid to lie down in such company, shot my snake dead."

Back in London, Sloane devoted himself to his major interests, medicine and natural history. *Catalogus Plantarum quae in insula Jamaica sponte proveniunt* was published in 1696 with the dedication to the Royal Society and to the College of Physicians. It called forth the highest praise from Ray and the other critics, whose seal of approval Sloane merited by the exact and detailed study he had set forth. Apparently he was not satisfied with the various degrees to his credit, or perhaps he felt that an English degree would further the success of an English doctor; whatever the reason, he worked for and received a degree of Doctor of Medicine from Oxford in July, 1701.

Thus the dawn of the eighteenth century in England found a man endowed with abilities far beyond the ordinary level, educated in the best schools of London and the

FLORALIA *Patrons of the Gentle Art*

Continent, widely traveled for his time, who stood as a patron of horticulture and promoter of science. For more than sixty years, Sir Hans practiced medicine, widened his interest in botany and its allied subjects and added to his collections. There was just cause for the Duchess to claim upon viewing the collection that she "had beheld many things odder than himself." Many jeers and sneers came from his contemporaries since Sloane was omnivorous and not at all discriminating. From the time of his boyhood days in Ireland, he had been gathering specimens and that was a day when "the possession of a taste for collecting insects was thought by able men of the world to be a strong presumption of lunacy."

During student days in France he had accumulated a quantity of unusual objects and the Jamaica voyage had provided the opportunity of adding many plant specimens. In addition, the magnificent collection of William Courten had come into Sir Hans's possession by the payment of the former's debts. John Evelyn had viewed the Courten collection in these words: "taken altogether, in all kinds doubtless one of the most perfect assemblage of rarities that can be anywhere seene . . . It consisted of miniatures, drawings, shells, insects, medailes, natural things, animals (of which divers, I think 100, were kept in glasses of spirits of wine) minerals, precious stones, vessells, curiousities in amber, chrystal, achat, &c., all being very perfect and rare in their kind, especially his books of birds, fish, flowers, and shells, drawn and miniatur'd to the life." Throughout his life, friends augmented his store by sending treasures from many parts of the world. Sloane was interested in and never spurned the amateurs in the field of botany and horticulture. His willingness to share his treasures with them, as well as with the more learned, is indicated by the following letter:

Sir Henry Goodricke to Sir Hans Sloane.
Ribstan, near Bouroughbridge, in Yorkshire, 1712/13
Sir,

The civilitys I have received from you do incourage me to give the trouble of a letter, and knowing you to be one who loves to incourage curiosity makes me hope that the subject of my letter won't be so disagreeable to you as to another. It is to desire of you that if among your rarities you have any number of seeds, nuts or kernells of foreign and rare trees especially those that are hardy I shall verily thankfully pay for 'em, my pleasure being to raise such things in hot beds and preserve 'em with care; and I would not rob you of any but what you have so many as you may readily spare a part to one who will as readily supply you again when any accident happens to yours, which I believe y^{rs} are more subject to near London than we are, here where I myself take the chief care of my curious trees. I have not yet been able to procure a tree of the true lotus (Zizyphus lotus), nor the larch tree, both which Mr. Evelyn says grow well in our climate, and may be raised from seed; these seeds and any other exotics I doubt not to raise, I mean trees, for smaller plants are too numerous for me to attend; if you could procure me a small tree of each of those kinds I w^d repay you with thanks, being S^r y^s obliged and humble servant,

H. GOODRICKE.

In 1722 he purchased the Chelsea Physick Garden and then made it over to the Court of the Apothecaries Company. When the great Swedish botanist, Charles Linnaeus, visited Sir Hans in 1736 he was taken to inspect the Chelsea Garden and here he was introduced to its first curator, Philip Miller.

Mark Catesby paid tribute to the botanist-physician when he dedicated his natural history of Carolina "To that great naturalist and promoter of science, Sir Hans Sloane, Bart. to whose goodness I attribute much of the success I had in this undertaking." George Edwards, the author of a *History of Birds* and *Gleanings from Natural History*, expressed his feeling of appreciation for the interest Sir Hans had shown him during the years when he was librarian of the College of Physicians, in these words: "After his retirement to Chelsea he requested it as a favour to him (though I embraced it as an honour done to myself) that I would visit him every week, in order to divert him for an hour or two, with the common news of the town, and with everything particular that should happen amongst his acquaintance of the Royal Society, and other ingenious gentlemen, many of whom I was weekly conversant with; ..." Edwards was faithful in his attendance on Sir Hans and felt much affection for him. When the old gentleman passed on, on January 11, 1753, Edwards confesses he had to leave him as Sir Hans's sufferings were so great that they were "beyond what I could bear."

Many honors were bestowed on Sir Hans during his life. He was made a Fellow of the French Academy of Sciences in 1708 and was honored in like manner by the Royal Society of Berlin. In 1727 he succeeded Sir Isaac Newton as President of the Royal Society in England. Sloane had the unique distinction of being the first medical practitioner to receive an hereditary title when he was made a baronet in 1716. Although appointed by Queen Anne as her personal physician, he apparently left little impress on the history of medicine. The only medical writing extant after his death was "An Account of a Medicine for soreness, weakness, and distemper of the Eyes." This medicine was made up of "tutty, Lapid Haematitis, best Aloes, and prepared Pearl, rubbed in a Porphyry mortar and mixed with Viper's Grease to make a liniment." He was made President of the College of Physicians in 1719, an office which he held for sixteen years.

The chief interest that posterity has in Sir Hans is in his collection which was the beginning of the British Museum. At the time of his death it was said to have contained over 160,000 specimens, including 334 volumes of dried plants, 50,000 books and 23,000 coins and medals. There were many things of no consequence among this vast conglomeration, but in the Sloane collection in the British Museum today, there is a large number of valuable coins, gems, minerals, cameos, and numerous books on scientific subjects.

FLORALIA *Patrons of the Gentle Art*

Sir Hans was a man of great wealth, and for many years before his death, it was expected that he would leave his collection as a gift to the country in which he had spent most of his life. When his will was read, however, he said his collection, which he valued at £80,000, was to be offered to the English government for £20,000. If Parliament failed to take the offer a similar one was to be made to the Academies of the Continental countries. If none of them purchased the collection as a whole, it was then to be sold in lots and the proceeds were to be turned over to his estate.

Neither the King nor Parliament was interested in setting aside money to buy the collection. The Sloane family was wealthy and it was generally felt that Sir Hans should have made his gift outright. Finally a lottery was designed to raise the money and by a procedure that was disgraceful and in a manner that was undignified, sufficient funds were secured to buy the collection as well as a house in which to store it. Its opening at Bloomsbury as the British Museum in 1759 was the beginning of one of the world's greatest treasure houses.

During Sir Hans's last years when he was too feeble to carry on active work, his mind must have wandered over the various fields of endeavor that he had fostered. It is natural to suppose that a longing or a wish to know who would follow him as guardian of his beloved natural history often formed itself in his waking thoughts. If Sir Hans could have known it, destiny was already shaping his successor, for on January 4, 1743, in Argyle Street, London, Joseph Banks had been born.

Banks came of distinguished ancestry and wealthy parents. His education was such as was given to boys of his social and financial level; first a tutor, then Harrow, then Eton. From accounts he was a normal, healthy boy, more fond of the outdoors than he was of books, but all told a satisfactory pupil. The awakening to an innate love of nature came suddenly. While walking by himself along a green lane where flowers were blooming on every side, he was struck with a sudden awareness of the wonder of it all and exclaimed: "How beautiful . . . it is surely more natural that I should be taught to know all these productions of nature in preference to Greek and Latin: but the latter is my father's command, and it is my duty to obey him: I will however make myself acquainted with all these different plants for my own pleasure and gratification." He set himself to learn all that he could about botany, and his sources of instructions were a copy of Gerard's *Herbal* and the old women who were employed by apothecaries as herb gatherers.

Predominating over all the other interests during the years he was at Oxford was his love of natural history. Dr. Sibthorp, the botanical professor, was not giving any lectures while Banks was in Christ Church. In fact, he gave only one lecture during the tenure of his professorship. It was said: "Every scientific object slept during the forty years that he held the post." Banks asked permission to have Mr. Israel Lyons come from Cambridge. This request was granted on condition that the students who composed the class should pay the cost of the visiting instructor.

Sir William Banks, father of Joseph, had died in 1761, leaving his son a large fortune. When the young man left Oxford, after taking an honorary degree there in 1763, instead of making a "grand tour" as was fashionable for one of his station, he resolved to pursue with intensity the study of natural history and to explore unknown countries in its interest.

In Joseph Banks occurred the remarkable and fortunate combination of wealth, desire to study, and leisure time, for few botanists were rich men and not many rich men were scientific students. During the years of his long life he devoted money, time, as well as his own energies, to the interest that had broken so suddenly into his life when he was a school boy. In 1766, accompanied by a friend, he made his first scientific expedition on a sailing vessel to Newfoundland, stopping to visit islands off the coast of Labrador. On this trip he laid the foundation of his splendid collection, although some valuable plants were lost when a storm washed them overboard on the homeward trip. The scientific world regarded the results of the Labrador trip with approval. They signified this by inviting Joseph Banks to make his first appearance at the Royal Society, which he did February 15, 1767. He gave himself freely during the latter years of his life to the affairs of this institution.

After his return Banks spent much of his time in Lincolnshire at his country place, Revesby Abbey. Believing as he did, like the poet Shenstone, that agriculture was a branch of botanical science, he considered his farming activities in the nature of laboratory experiments. He liked to roam about the estate and was extremely fond of fishing. On one of his angling expeditions quite by chance he made the acquaintance of Lord Sandwich, who afterwards was made one of the Lords of the Admiralty. The outgrowth of this friendship had a significant bearing on the world of science, in that Lord Sandwich's department gave cooperation to the voyages that Banks later promoted and participated in with such great success.

In 1768 opportunity came for a real adventure. From the time of George III's accession to the throne he had been interested in enlarging geographical science. Three expeditions had already been sent out, and a fourth was being planned for the purpose of observing the transit of the planet Venus over the disc of the sun. The Royal Society was enthusiastic over the proposed journey; Banks by his participation in the affairs of the society became interested in the voyage and obtained permission to become a member of the party, fitting out the ship at his own expense. He was determined that natural history should benefit by this excursion. His staff on the voyage consisted of Dr. Solander, the sub-librarian of the British Museum, two artists, a secretary and four servants. On April 26, 1768, the good ship "Endeavour" under Captain James Cook set sail from Plymouth Sound. She was gone three years and in that time she had sailed around the globe and touched many places, Tierra del Fuego, New Zealand, Otaheite, Batavia, Cape of Good Hope, and St. Helena, among them.

The voyage was successful beyond expectation. In addition to the observation of the transit of Venus, a great store was added to geographical knowledge, and Cook showed himself to be a first class captain in the unknown waters. Banks, together with Solander and the other members of his staff, by faithful and untiring efforts, collected many botanical treasures and carefully recorded the native haunts of the plants. The result of their work was the contribution to natural history of a vast amount of information about tropical and subtropical flora. The breadfruit, which Banks discovered in Otaheite, so impressed him as a valuable food product that he mentally resolved to transplant it nearer home. He made this resolution during hours spent walking under the shade of the trees. This, with the cocoanut palm, furnished two of the chief articles of diet for the crew while the "Endeavour" sailed in tropical waters. Observations were made of birds, fish and animals, as well as plants, and about the strangest sight that the company had to report was the "kangooroo," which they saw in New Zealand. The herbarium, collected during this voyage, is now in the Natural History Museum in South Kensington.

Captain Cook made two other important voyages in the interest of extending natural science. Banks was anxious to accompany him and was willing at his own expense to equip the vessels with elaborate accommodations. But jealousy crept in and there was a feeling that the young naturalist and not the ship's company had received the glory after the first journey. So many impediments were put in the way that Banks was obliged to abandon plans for further trips. In spite of his disappointment he did all he could to promote the voyages.

Honors came to this man who gave of himself so unselfishly. He was given a baronetcy by the King in 1781. Just as Sir Hans Sloane, the leading patron of the natural sciences during the first half of the century, was made President of the Royal Society, so likewise on Sir Joseph Banks, who played the role as Chief Guardian during the remainder of this period, was bestowed the same honor, on December 7, 1778. From this time until his death, in 1820, he carried on enthusiastically the duties of this important and influential office.

During the last quarter of the century Sir Joseph promoted expeditions of many plant explorers and collectors whose adventures entailed danger as well as glory. Francis Masson, who worked in Kew Gardens under Aiton for several years, was selected by Banks as the chief collector. He made three journeys, in what was then quick succession; one to the Cape of Good Hope, one in company with Thunberg to the interior of Africa, and another to a point 500 miles north of Cape Town. His labors were rewarded since he brought home for Kew Gardens hundreds of new plants in which there were some notable treasures. Masson spent the rest of his days traveling in the interest of plant collecting, and Banks remained his firm friend and counselor until his death occurred on one of his collecting expeditions.

Banks was interested not only in the explorers and collectors who belonged to his own country, but he kept in frequent communication with naturalists in other parts of the world. To the East India Company, which was endeavoring to improve the food supply of the people under its supervision, he gave freely of his time and knowledge. In addition, he corresponded with Lord Cornwallis, who had been sent as governor to Bengal in 1786, and advised him in his efforts to transplant the sago palm, as well as the Persian date palm into the province over which he ruled. During Colonel Kidd's struggle to found the Calcutta Botanic Garden, Banks gave valuable counsel, and the pioneer students of Indian Flora, Dr. Koenig, a Dane who had studied under Linnaeus, and Dr. William Roxburgh, were in constant communication with him. These men, as well as many others, benefited by his friendly interest and knowledge, and the money that Sir Joseph so willingly bestowed on those who seriously pursued the expansion of natural history.

The best remembered expedition in the name of plant collecting which Sir Joseph sponsored was that of Captain William Bligh in command of the "Bounty." This expedition was planned with the idea of collecting breadfruit trees for transplantation in the West Indies. Banks wrote instructions for the gardener, David Nelson. He wrote a similarly carefully drawn up document for every new collector who was about to embark on a voyage. The instructions began: "As the sole object of Government in chartering this vessel in our service at a very considerable expense is to furnish the West Indian Islands with the Bread-fruit and other valuable productions of the East, the master and crew of her must not think it a grievance to give up the best part of her accommodations for that purpose. The difficulty of carrying plants by sea is very great: a small sprinkling of salt water, or of the salt dew which fills the air even in a moderate gale, will inevitably destroy them if not immediately washed off with fresh water. It is necessary therefore that the cabin be appropriated to the sole purpose of making a kind of greenhouse, and the key of it given to the custody of the gardener; and that in case of cold weather in going round the Cape a stove be provided, by which it may be kept in a temperature equal to that of the intertropical countries." He instructed the captain further: "Her first destination will be New Zealand, where she is to take on board two tubs of flax plants. From thence she is to proceed to the Society Isles, where she must stay till the gardener has produced a full stock of Bread-fruit trees; and if Otaheite, which will probably be visited first, should not supply a sufficient number of such as are of a proper age for transplanting, she must proceed to Imao, Maitea, Husheine, Ulietea, and Bolabola, and stay till enough are procured."

The well known story of mutiny on the "Bounty" has furnished material for many romantic and adventurous sea tales. In spite of the disastrous failure Bligh was again appointed to carry out the commission. He was put in command of the "Providence" which set sail in 1791. After a long voyage he safely landed a cargo of three hundred breadfruit plants in Jamaica and the same number in some of the other islands of the West Indies. Thus was Sir Joseph's resolve, made on his voyage with Captain Cook in the "Endeavour," ultimately carried out.

CHAPTER V

America: A Floral Hunting Ground

FROM THE TIME AMERICA WAS DISCOVERED, the plant life of this new world had been impressive and important to explorers. The earliest records of travelers show that they had seen with pleasure what nature had placed along their route. Eagerly they brought back to the mother country Indian corn, sassafras, and the sweet potato, which were received with interest at first and finally with enthusiasm. For example, the sassafras root was found to make a drink at once delicious and also useful for its medicinal properties. The tea became so popular in England that sailors, when in America, would steal food from the ship's mess to trade to the Indians for the roots. With increased exploration and travel, the plant life of America became more and more important to the mother country.

Although separated from England by a hazardous voyage varying from one to three months, America was not untouched by the new philosophy of life which pervaded English thought and the English garden world during the eighteenth century. To America, too, was carried the idea of a life close to nature as the most satisfactory

FLORALIA *A Floral Hunting Ground*

way to the pursuit of happiness. This way of life found a staunch advocate in Saint John de Crèvecoeur (1735-1813), a Frenchman, who adopted the new world for his own and became "an humble American planter and a simple cultivator of the Earth." He repaid with interest and joy what the simple life in America had given him in his twelve essays, written in 1782 under the title *Letters from an American Farmer*. "After all," he observed, "why should not a farmer be allowed to make use of his mental faculties as well as others? Because a man works is he not to think, and if he thinks usefully, why should he not in his leisure hours set down his thoughts? I have composed many a good sermon as I followed my plough." His *Letters* picture in a very delightful and accurate manner the peace, charm, and fulfillment of desire that is found in rural life. One of these letters is of greatest importance to the follower of natural history, for it contains a most interesting account of the notable American naturalist, John Bartram (1699-1777), and devotes considerable space to the expression of his ideas and to a description of his work.

This account is in letter eleven, entitled "From Mr. Iw-n Al-z, a Russian gentleman; describing the visit he paid at my request to Mr. John Bertram, the celebrated Pennsylvania botanist." Crèvecoeur's "correspondent" wrote:

"... let us together, agreeable to your desire, pay a visit to Mr. John Bertram, the first botanist, in this new hemisphere: become such by a native impulse of disposition. It is to this simple man that America is indebted for several useful discoveries, and the knowledge of many new plants. I had been greatly prepossessed in his favour by the extensive correspondence which I knew he held with the most eminent Scotch and French Botanists; I knew also that he had been honoured with that of Queen Ulrica of Sweden.

"His house is small, but decent; there was something peculiar in its first appearance, which seemed to distinguish it from those of his neighbours: a small tower in the middle of it, not only helped to strengthen it but afforded convenient room for a staircase. Every disposition of the fields, fences, and trees, seemed to bear the marks of perfect order and regularity, which in rural affairs, always indicate a prosperous industry."

Mr. Iw-n Al-z describes his meeting with the great botanist thus:

"An elderly looking man, with wide trowsers and a large leather apron on, looking at me said: 'My name is Bertram, dost thee want me?' Sir, I am come on purpose to converse with you, if you can be spared from your labour. 'Very easily (he answered). I direct and advise more than I work.' We walked toward the house, where he made me take a chair while he went to put on clean clothes, after which he returned and sat down by me."

After an exchange of civilities, an interesting give and take of ideas and after they had consumed an "honest country dinner" the conversation of the two men, reported in such admirable detail, turned to Bartram's own work. His own words, expressing his debt to the great Swedish

FLORALIA *A Floral Hunting Ground*

naturalist and giving the origin of his interest in botany, follow:

"Friend Iwan, as I make no doubt that thee understandest the Latin tongue, read this kind epistle which the good Queen of Sweden, *Ulrica,* sent me a few years ago. Good woman! that she should think in her palace at Stockholm of poor John Bertram, on the banks of the Schuylkill; appeareth to me very strange. Not in the least, dear Sir; you are the first man whose name as a botanist hath done honour to America; it is very natural at the same time to imagine, that so extensive a continent must contain many curious plants and trees; is it then surprising to see a princess, fond of useful knowledge, descend sometimes from the throne, to walk in the gardens of Linnaeus? 'Tis to the directions of that learned man (said Mr. Bertram) that I am indebted for the method which has led me to the knowledge I now possess; the science of botany is so diffusive, that a proper thread is absolutely wanted to conduct the beginner. Pray, Mr. Bertram, when did you imbibe the first wish to cultivate the science of botany;

" 'Well, then, I'll tell thee: One day I was very busy in holding my plough (for thee seest that I am but a ploughman) and being weary I ran under the shade of a tree to repose myself. I cast my eyes on a *daisy,* I plucked it mechanically and viewed it with more curiosity than common country farmers are wont to do; and observed therein very many distinct parts, some perpendicular, some horizontal. *What a shame, said my mind, or something that inspired my mind, that thee shouldest have employed so*

FLORALIA *A Floral Hunting Ground*

many years in tilling the earth and destroying so many flowers and plants, without being acquainted with their structures and their uses! This seeming inspiration suddenly awakened my curiosity, for these were not thoughts to which I had been accustomed. I returned to my team, but this new desire did not quit my mind; I mentioned it to my wife, who greatly discouraged me from prosecuting my new scheme, as she called it; I was not opulent enough, she said, to dedicate much of my time to studies and labours which might rob me of that portion of it which is the only wealth of the American farmer. However her prudent caution did not discourage me; I thought about it continually, at supper, in bed, and wherever I went. At last I could not resist the impulse; for on the fourth day of the following week, I hired a man to plough for me, and went to Philadelphia. Though I knew not what book to call for, I ingeniously told the bookseller my errand, who provided me with such as he thought best, and a Latin grammar beside. Next I applied to a neighbouring schoolmaster, who in three months taught me Latin enough to understand Linnaeus, which I purchased afterward. Then I began to botanize all over my farm; in a little time I became acquainted with every vegetable that grew in my neighbourhood; and next ventured into Maryland, living among the Friends; in proportion as I thought myself more learned I proceeded farther, and by a steady application of several years I have acquired a pretty general knowledge of every plant and tree to be found in our continent. In process of time I was applied to from the old

FLORALIA *A Floral Hunting Ground*

countries, whither I every year send my collections. Being now made easy in my circumstances, I have ceased to labour, and am never so happy as when I see and converse with my friends. If among the many plants or shrubs I am acquainted with, there are any thee wantest to send to thy native country, I will cheerfully procure them, and give thee moreover whatever directions thee mayest want."

Thus Crèvecoeur paints a picture of that classical figure among early botanists. Inspired by a deep reverence for natural history and especially botany, John Bartram zealously labored to discover the plant treasures of the vast and unexplored continent on which he lived. At the instigation of his English friend, Peter Collinson, he began about the year 1730 to collect seeds and plants. These he sent to Collinson and other men of like interest in England and on the Continent. It was Peter Collinson who was instrumental in the practical side of the transaction, i.e., in obtaining from Philip Miller, Lord Petre and others the sum of 30 guineas to be paid annually to Bartram in return for the specimens which he sent them. Bartram must have been possessed of great energy for after collecting the plants he wrote long letters describing his finds and giving many valuable notes on their properties.

The lady's slippers were very pleasing to his European friends, and they constantly asked for more varieties. The little white atamasco lily and "red flowering lillies" also excited enthusiasm. Mosses were very interesting curiosities and seeds were shipped by the dozen boxes. A flowering tree, which was a never ending source of pleasure and

FLORALIA *A Floral Hunting Ground*

wonder to the European gardeners, was the *Magnolia grandiflora* which originally came from South Carolina, where it attained tremendous size. This was hopefully exported to England, and though English soil and climate were not conducive to tremendous growth, the *Magnolia* flowered satisfactorily.

The letters which passed between Bartram and Collinson have been referred to in an earlier chapter. In addition to Collinson, Bartram constantly corresponded with Sir Hans Sloane, who presented the collector with a silver cup as a reward for some unusual plants. Other correspondents were John James Dillenius, J. F. Gronovius, the great Dutch botanist, Philip Miller, Dr. Sibthorp, Dr. Solander, Dr. John Hill, as well as many others prominent in the European botanical world. His letters to James Logan, Colonel W. Byrd, Colonel Custis, and Dr. Alexander Garden show that he also kept in touch with men of like interest in his own country. This voluminous correspondence is worthwhile and historically valuable as a record of early eighteenth century plant life, for Bartram, according to one of his biographers, "detected more undescribed plants than any of his contemporaries in our country."

In addition to his wide explorations and extensive collections, he established a Botanic Garden, the first institution of its kind in the Western World. It was located a short distance from Philadelphia on the Schuylkill River. In this beautiful situation he successfully transplanted most of the treasures which he had observed and here he tended with much affection the plants that he gathered

CRIMSON PENNSYLVANIA MARTAGON

FLORALIA *A Floral Hunting Ground*

in his wanderings "from New England to near Georgia, and from the Sea Coast to Lake Ontario."

The garden, loved so much by him, was doubtless indirectly responsible for his death. When the British army was fighting its way from the Brandywine to Philadelphia, the fear seized him that the beloved child of his creation would be in the line of march of the oncoming soldiers and this was more than the old man could stand; death came to him on September 22, 1777. However, the garden was spared. Perhaps the soldiers respected the home of one who had been "Botanist Royal for the British Colonies," or possibly it was respect for a man who had a deep reverence for God and an abiding love of nature.

John Bartram was the first of a line of important botanists who did valuable work in Pennsylvania during the eighteenth century. During the same period there was James Logan, who proved himself by his experiments and essays to be a man of profound scientific ability. His essay, *Experimenta et Meletemata de Plantarum generatione,* which was published at Leyden in 1739, set forth his observations upon the pollen grains and illustrated Linnaeus's theory of the sexes of plants. John Bartram handed his torch, along with excellent botanical instruction, to his son William (1739-1823) who carried it in such a worthy manner that for over a hundred years the two of them shed much botanical light on America. Though "Billy," as he was affectionately called by his father, did much of his work in the South, he actually spent most of his life in his native state.

FLORALIA *A Floral Hunting Ground*

John Bartram not only corresponded with many of the better known botanists of his day but when Peter Kalm, the Swedish naturalist and pupil of Linnaeus, came to this country in the year 1748, there was opportunity for personal friendship and association that was mutually beneficial. Soon after his arrival in this country, Kalm made the following note: "In the morning I went . . . to the Country Seat of Mr. Bartram which is four English miles to the South of Philadelphia. I had therefore the first opportunity here of getting an exact Knowledge of the State of the Country which was a plain covered with all Kinds of trees with deciduous leaves. . . ." Kalm spent three years in this country. During that time he made his headquarters around Philadelphia, but he traveled from Pennsylvania through New Jersey and New York to Quebec and back to Philadelphia through western Pennsylvania. He was a keen observer and throughout his journeys he faithfully chronicled his observations, so that when his *Travels into North America* was published in 1753, another very valuable record was added to botanical literature of the time.

While the Swedish visitor frankly acknowledged that he found much of interest in this country, he was not willing to admit that what the colonies offered was in any way superior to what he had been accustomed to in Europe. He made the following interesting comment: "The Trees of this Country have the same qualities as its inhabitants. For the Ships which are built of American wood, are by no means equal in point of strength to those which are built in Europe. This is what nobody attempts to con-

FLORALIA *A Floral Hunting Ground*

tradict." Again he said: "Several ships are annually built of American Oak (in Philadelphia) in the docks, which are made in several parts of the town, yet they can by no means be put in comparison with those built of European Oak in point of goodness and duration."

There were contemporaneous botanists in each geographical division of the new country. Dr. Cadwallader Colden, who was much engrossed in the turbulent political affairs of the colonies in the middle of the century, became an able student of the plant life that grew around his home, Coldenham, which was situated on the Hudson River above New York. Dr. John Torrey said: "The earliest treatise on the Botany of New York was the *Plantae Coldenhamiae* of Governor Colden, published in the Act of the Royal Society of Upsala for the year 1744. It is an account of the plants growing spontaneously in the neighborhood of Coldenham, in Orange County, and embraces only the first twelve classes of the Linnaean system." In New England, Reverend Manasseh Cutler seems to have made the first scientific study of plants for his section when he published *Plants of New England* during the latter part of the century.

What John Bartram was doing in Pennsylvania "My friend, John Clayton, the great botanist of America," so called by Peter Collinson, was doing in Virginia. Clayton was thorough and practical in his work; he made a botanical survey of Orange County and collected and described numberless specimens of Virginia plants. He sent them to Holland to Professor Gronovius, who, with the help of

FLORALIA *A Floral Hunting Ground*

Linnaeus, living in that country at the time, gave them proper characters and descriptions and arranged them according to the sexual system. So, when *Flora Virginica* was published at Leyden in 1739, it was, according to William Darlington, the first systematic enumeration of North American plants. Clayton's friends felt that he never received his share of credit for this volume since most of it was given to Gronovius. It can be readily understood, however, that the basic work done by a mere naturalist in the lowly colonies should have been overshadowed by an editor so well known in a full-fledged European country.

Thomas Jefferson, himself an eminent gardener, later in the century paid tribute to Dr. John Clayton in his *Notes on the State of Virginia:* ". . . for an enumeration and scientific description (of trees and plants) I must refer to the *Flora Virginica* of our great botanist, Dr. John Clayton, published by Gronovius at Leyden. This accurate observer was a native and resident of this State, passed a long life in exploring and describing its plants, and is supposed to have enlarged the botanical catalogue as much as almost any one who has lived."

Another interesting record of the natural life of Virginia in the eighteenth century was left by Reverend Andrew Burnaby in his *Travels Through the Middle Settlements in North America in the Years 1759-1760*, published in London by Payne in 1775. Burnaby wrote: "Besides trees and flowers of an ordinary nature, the woods produce myrtles, cedars, cypresses, sugar trees, firs of dif-

FLORALIA *A Floral Hunting Ground*

ferent sorts, and no less than seven or eight kinds of oak; they are likewise adorned and beautified with red flowering maples, sassafras-trees, dog-woods, acacias, red-buds, scarlet-flowering chestnuts, fringe-trees, flowering poplars, umbrellas, magnolias, yellow jasamines, chamoedaphnes, pacoons, atamusco lillies, May-apples, and innumerable other sorts; so that one may reasonably assert that no country ever appeared with greater elegence or beauty."

Another worker in Virginia was Dr. John Mitchell who had come to that colony early in the century, collecting widely throughout its territory. From his writing it appears that he was scientific in his observations, for in one paper he suggested thirty new genera of Virginia plants.

If one judges by the number of eminent botanists who hunted in South Carolina, that section of the country must have offered an unusually rich flora. The earliest observer of natural life in this colony was John Lawson, a Scotchman, who came into the Carolinas as a surveyor in 1700. He met a cruel death in 1712 at the hands of the Tuscarora Indians, but lived long enough to write one of the earliest histories of the Carolinas, and his account of the plant and animal life is therefore valuable.

The title of this volume was *A New Voyage to Carolina Containing the exact description and Natural History of that Country: together with the Present State thereof. And a Journal of a thousand miles travel'd thro' Several Nations of Indians, Giving a Particular Account of their Customs, Manners. etc. by John Lawson. Gent. Surveyor General of North Carolina.* The work was printed in

81

FLORALIA *A Floral Hunting Ground*

London in the year 1709, and was dedicated to the "True and Absolute Lords-Proprietors of the Province of Carolina in America." Following the dedication is Lawson's impression of life as it could be lived in the province: "I here present your Lordships with a Description of your own Country, for the most part of her Natural Dress and therefore less vitiated with fraud and Luxury. A Country whose Inhabitants may enjoy a Life of the Greatest Ease and Satisfaction and pass away their Hours in Solid Contentment."

In the preface, he deplored the fact that the majority of Englishmen who came to the colony were a mediocre lot: " 'Tis a great misfortune, that most of our Travellers, who go into this vast Continent in America, are persons of the Meaner sort, and generally of a very slender education: who being hired by the merchants to trade amongst the Indians, in which voyages they often spend several years, are yet at their return incapable of giving any reasonable account of what they met with in these remote parts; Tho' the country abound with Curiosities worthy a nice observation. In this point, I think, the French out-strip us." He pays tribute to the character and intelligence of the French missionaries who had preceded him in this country.

His *Journal of a Thousand Miles Travel'd* was a diary he kept during a journey begun on December 28, 1700, and his travels, which carried him from Charlestown into North Carolina, were in the company of "six Englishmen, three Indian men and one Woman." Lawson gave full and

FLORALIA *A Floral Hunting Ground*

accurate descriptions of the "vegetables" and "spontaneous shrubs," found along his path of travel. Like so many other early travelers in this country, he was tremendously impressed by the oaks. He noticed also "cedars, two sorts" and "holly, two sorts" and wrote at length upon the youpon which he found growing most plentifully along the coast. "It grows the most like box of any vegetable that I know, being very like it in leaf, only dented and somewhat fatter." According to his journal, the Carolinas abounded with luxuriant plant life.

While John Bartram was botanizing through his section of the country, and collecting material for his European friends as well as for his own garden, eager explorers were likewise employed in other sections. At the same time, a young Englishman, the botanic peer of Bartram, named Mark Catesby (1679-1749), was working farther south.

Catesby, who was born with a love of natural history, made a voyage to Virginia where he had relatives. There, he said, it "Suited most with my Convenience to go to, where I arrived the 23^d April 1712." He spent seven years in that colony, where "I chiefly gratified my Inclination in observing and admiring the various Productions of those Countries." During this time he sent to a number of his interested friends in England some dried as well as living specimens of plants and a portion of the most valuable he sent in tubs of earth.

When he returned to his native land in 1719 he became known, through his collections, to William Sherard, that

FLORALIA *A Floral Hunting Ground*

celebrated botanist, and to Sir Hans Sloane, Bart., then President of the Royal Society and of the College of Physicians. These and other friends and patrons urged Catesby to revisit America; they not only gave him encouragement, but they also gave him money for the second voyage to the new country, for they realized that he had the ability to seek out and to describe properly the unusual and interesting plant and animal life. As a result, he left England in 1722, and tells his own story in the following manner: "I set out . . . directly for Carolina . . . its productions being very little known, except what barely related to Commerce, such as Rice, Pitch and Tar; was thought the most proper Place to search and describe the Productions of; accordingly I arriv'd in Carolina 23^d May 1722 after a pleasant tho' not a short Passage . . .

"Upon my arrival at *Charles Town*, I waited on General *Nicholson,* then Governor of that Province, who received me with much kindness, and continued his Favours . . .

"As I arrived at the beginning of the Summer, I unexpectedly found this country possessed not only with all the Animals and Vegetables of *Virginia,* but abounding with even a greater variety. The Inhabited Parts of *Carolina* extend West from the Sea about sixty Miles, and almost the whole length of the coast, being a level, low country. In these Parts I continued the first Year, searching after, collecting and describing the Animals and Plants. I then went to the Upper uninhabited Parts of the Country, and continued at and about Fort Moore, a small

FLORALIA *A Floral Hunting Ground*

Fortress on the Banks of the River *Savanna*, which runs from thence a Course of 300 Miles down to the Sea, and is about the same Distance from its Source, in the Mountains.

"I was much delighted to see Nature differ in these Upper Parts, and to find here abundance of things not to be seen in the Lower parts of the country. This encouraged me to take several Journeys with the Indians higher up the Rivers, towards the Mountains, which afforded not only a Succession of new vegetable Appearances, but the most delightful Prospects imaginable, besides the Diversion of Hunting Buffello's, Bears, Panthers, and other wild Beasts. In these Excursions I employed an *Indian* to carry my Box, in which, besides paper and material for Painting, I put dry'd Specimens of Plants, Seeds, &c. as I gather'd them. To the Hospitality and Assistance of these friendly *Indians*, I am much indebted, for I not only subsisted on what they shot, but their first Care was to erect a bark hut, at the Approach of Rain, to keep me and my Cargo from Wet."

Catesby spent nearly three years on the continent. He wandered through Carolina, Georgia and Florida studying the plant and animal life and making drawings as he went along. "As I was not bred a Painter I hope some faults in Perspective, and other Niceties, may be more readily excused; for I humbly conceive Plants, and other Things done in a Flat, tho' exact manner, may serve the Purpose of Natural History, better in some Measure, than in a more bold and Painterlike Way. In designing the Plants, I

FLORALIA *A Floral Hunting Ground*

always did them while fresh and just gathered: and the Animals, particularly the Birds, I painted them while alive (except a very few) and gave them their Gestures peculiar to every kind of Bird, and where it would admit of, I have adapted the Birds to those Plants on which they fed, or have any Relation to. Fish, which do not retain their Colours when out of their Element, I painted at different times, having a succession of them Procur'd while the former lost their Colours: I do not pretend to have had this advantage in all, for some kinds I saw not plenty of, and of others I never saw above one or two. Reptiles will live many Months without Sustenance; so that I had no difficulty in Painting them while living."

After having spent three years in the manner which is related here he went to the Bahama Islands where his principal studies were devoted to fish. Upon his return to England in 1726, he was gratified at having his labors approved by "gentlemen most skilled in the learning of Nature." Catesby, encouraged by the approval he received, then settled himself to the task of preparing his notes and drawings which were finally published as: *The Natural History of Carolina, Florida, and the Bahama Islands: Containing the figures of* BIRDS, BEASTS, FISHES, SERPENTS, INSECTS, *and* PLANTS: *particularly the forest-trees, shrubs, and other plants, not hitherto described, or very incorrectly figured by authors. Together with their descriptions in English and French . . . To the whole, is prefixed a new and correct Map of the Countries treated of—London, Printed at the expense of the author, 1731-42.*

FLORALIA *A Floral Hunting Ground*

This work was dedicated to the Queen and a list of the encouragers follows the dedication page. Among the names were those of Mr. John Bartram of Pennsylvania, Mr. George Edwards, Mr. Robert Furber, the Honorable Lieutenant General F. Nicholson, Governor of South Carolina, the Right Honorable the Lord Petre. Volume I, published in 1731, was devoted to birds and plant life. Each plate pictures a bird and a plant, the plant forming either a perch or a background for the bird. Two columns of notes are on the page opposite the plate and descriptions of the bird are at the top of the page in English and French; below, the plant is described in the same languages. For example, Plate 27, showing the "Mock-Bird" perched on the limb of a pink dogwood tree, is particularly pleasing and significant: "We call it the Mock-Bird from its wonderful mocking and imitating the notes of all Birds, from humming bird to the eagle. From March till August it sings incessantly day and night with the greatest variety of notes." The white dogwood, he said, grew in all sections, but he found only one pink dogwood and that one grew in Virginia. Plate 45 pictures the blue linnet against a pink trillium and though interesting it is not well proportioned. Another shows the humming bird and the trumpet flower.

While Volume II, published in 1743, is given over almost entirely to fish and serpents, there are, however, some notices of plants; the magnolia or laurel tree of Carolina and the flytraps or *Sarracenia* being pictured very well. The importance of the work is shown by the number

FLORALIA *A Floral Hunting Ground*

of editions through which it went. A revised one, edited by Mr. George Edwards, was published in 1748, a German one in Nuremberg in 1756, and another English one in 1771. There was also an edition in French. For over two hundred years the *Natural History* has held a place of prime importance as a work on botany, since it contains the earliest descriptions and figures of a number of plants as well as animals and birds of the section to which it refers.

The work next in importance, *The Hortus Britanno-Americanus, or a Curious Collection of Trees and Shrubs, the Produce of the British Colonies in North America* was a very significant work and is dealt with in more detail in the following chapter. The last book of importance by Catesby, *The Migration of Birds,* was published in 1747.

Mark Catesby died in London on December 23, 1749. He was honored by the Dutch naturalist, Gronovius, who named a genus of plants *Catesbaea* in his memory.

About the middle of the century, there came into South Carolina Dr. Alexander Garden (1728-1791), who like Lawson was also a native of Scotland. In him is another interesting combination of physician and botanist. During the thirty years spent in the practice of his profession in Charleston, he also devoted much time to the study of botany and found great joy in the revelations of nature. Dr. Garden had received an excellent classical as well as medical education in his home country. In order to augment his knowledge of the natural sciences, he traveled in the new country and made scientific observations of the plant life. He left a number of treatises; one was *An Ac-*

FLORALIA *A Floral Hunting Ground*

count of the Pink Root with its Uses as a Vermifuge, *published in 1764. Dr. Garden was made a Fellow in the Royal Society in 1772 and when he went to England to live during his latter years, he was made a vice-president of this organization. Linnaeus memorialized Dr. Garden by naming a fragrant flower, *Gardenia*, in his honor.

In the year 1773, William Bartram (1739-1823), son of John, who has been referred to earlier in this chapter, came to Charleston, South Carolina. Under the patronage of Dr. Fothergill of London, he spent five years traveling through the South for the purpose of discovering "rare and useful productions chiefly in the vegetable kingdom."

Bartram was a faithful chronicler and kept a diary from the time he left Charleston, his starting point. "Early in the morning," he writes, "we mounted our horses, and in two days arrived in Savannah . . . The day following we sat off for Augusta." From Augusta he went back to Savannah, then into Florida, and as far west as Mobile. On his return from this point, while coming through Georgia, he had the good fortune to observe a new flowering shrub. He remarked: "On first observing the fructification and habit of this tree, I was inclined to believe it a species of *Gordonia*, but afterwards upon stricter examination, and comparing its flowers and fruit with those of *Gordonia lasianthus*, I presently found striking characteristics abundantly sufficient to separate it from that genus, and to establish it the head of a new tribe, which we have honored with the name of the illustrious Dr. Benjamin Franklin, *Franklinia alatamaha*."

FLORALIA *A Floral Hunting Ground*

Bartram "sat upon" his return homeward from Charleston. He carries his readers through every step of the journey and he faithfully records the change in the topography as well as in the vegetation as he traveled northward. When almost home he came upon "insuperable embarrassment, the river being but half froze over," but after a couple of days, he managed to cross it, and arrived at his father's house in January, 1778.

The outgrowth of the diary he kept on his travels was published in Philadelphia in 1791 as *Travels through North and South Carolina, Georgia, East and West Florida, the Cherokee Country, the Extensive territories of the Muscogulges or Creek Confederacy and the Country of the Choctaws, Containing an account of the Soil and Natural productions of those regions, together with observations on the Manners of the Indians. Embellished with Copper Plates.*

While William Bartram was arranging his *Travels* for publication, Thomas Walter (1740-1789), was likewise occupied with *Flora Caroliniana* which was published in London in 1788, the year before he died. Walter, who was born in Hampshire, England, came to South Carolina in early manhood and settled on the Santee River, where he spent the rest of his life. Though the affairs of his plantation occupied much of his time, nevertheless, his favorite leisure pursuit was botanizing. That he was a man of profound erudition, well grounded in the classics, and unusually gifted as a botanist, is shown by his work *Flora*

FLORALIA *A Floral Hunting Ground*

Caroliniana. Secundum systema vegetabilium, perillustris Linnaei Digesta;...Auctore Thomas Walter, Agricula ...Londini, Sumptibus J. Fraser, 1788. This work, done entirely in Latin, was dedicated to Gulielmo Pitcairn. According to William Maxon, in his pamphlet on Thomas Walter, *Flora Caroliniana* is the first descriptive treatise upon the flowering plants of any definite region in Eastern North America, using the binomial system of nomenclature.

One feels sure that Walter's love for his plants was commensurate with his botanical knowledge, for in the inscription on his tombstone is carved: "At his desire he was buried on this spot once the garden in which were cultivated most of the plants of his *Flora Caroliniana."*

There is a very interesting connection between Thomas Walter and John Fraser, a Scotchman, who spent a large part of his time in America during the last twenty years of the century. He came into South Carolina in 1786 and when he returned to England in 1788 he carried with him Walter's manuscript which he published that year at his own expense. John Fraser was very famous as a botanical collector, and he was an associate of Michaux as well as of Walter. During the time that he was in America he made many valuable contributions to English gardens.

Any record of plant explorers in South Carolina would be incomplete if it did not include the name of André Michaux (1746-1802), who was sent there on a collecting mission by the French Government soon after the American Revolution. For almost a century, plant life from

FLORALIA *A Floral Hunting Ground*

North America had become increasingly important in Europe, and it was felt that trees from the new country would be a valuable addition to the royal plantations of France. André Michaux was commissioned to go to America to find and to send home those trees and plants he considered most valuable.

He traveled in America from 1785 to 1796. The year 1787 brought him into South Carolina where the natural conditions as he found them aroused such enthusiasm that he decided Charleston was the place for his headquarters. A nursery was established on the Ashley River. Michaux traveled far and wide and cheerfully faced every hardship and peril of the wilderness and frontier in collecting the rare trees and plants which he sent back to Charleston as stock for his nursery. The specimens were later sent from the nursery to France. Giving freely in return for what was given him, Michaux was the first to introduce into America many of the valuable plants from Europe, and shared his knowledge of agriculture and botany with the people whom he met in his travels. The Agricultural Society of Charleston recognized the value of his services by making him a member of their organization. Two great books in which he recorded his observations of American plant life were, *L'Histoire des Chênes de l'Amérique* and *Flora boreali-americana* which were published in 1801 and 1803 respectively.

Michaux traveled more widely in America than any other plant explorer at the time that he lived. During his travels he kept a diary which was presented to the Ameri-

FLORALIA *A Floral Hunting Ground*

can Philosophical Society by his son, F. André Michaux, in 1824. Unfortunately the record of the first part of his stay in America had been lost. The first record is dated Thursday, 19 April, 1787, at Charleston, South Carolina. Just as William Bartram did, Michaux first traveled to Augusta, Georgia, and he said of it: "La ville d'Augusta est une des plus agréablement situées de toute l'Am." Michaux went from Augusta into the northwestern section of South Carolina and to his delight he found the *Kalmia latifolia* in abundance. During the next three years he traveled as far north as Canada and as far west as Kentucky. He was faithful to his diary, which always included long lists of plants.

Perhaps the way had been cleared by Catesby, the Bartrams, and other fearless pioneers, but Michaux was equal to the opportunities, as well as the hardships, and he will be remembered as a valuable contributor to the knowledge of North American plant life at the end of the eighteenth century.

CHAPTER VI

Worthy Volumes About Trees

AMONG THE MANY IMPORTANT VOLUMES on horticulture which appeared in the eighteenth century, there were a number which dealt almost entirely with trees. Earlier in the century considerable attention had been paid to flowers, gardens in general, and landscaping. Trees had been touched upon only incidentally in respect to their part in completing the landscape picture or providing shade in pleasure gardens. A few of these worthy volumes appeared during the first half of the century. However, most of them came in the latter part and a few bespeak the controversies that were bringing discordance and animation into the garden world.

A number of the books in question had English origin. One of the earliest publications (1740) was that of Christopher Gray, a member of the Society of Gardeners. This work displayed a print of the *Magnolia altissima* and included a catalogue of some seventy-three American trees and shrubs "that will endure the climate of England." About the *Magnolia altissima,* Gray wrote: "The Trunks of these Trees are frequently three feet in diameter, and of

FLORÁLIA *Worthy Volumes about Trees*

a proportionable height they retain their leaves all the Winter. The flowers are white and fragrant, the colour of the cone or seed vessel is red with a mixture of green, and Nature dischargeth the many scarlet seeds hanging from the cone by white threds. This short description with the figure of Flower and Seed vessel here exhibited gives an idea I hope Sufficient to determine it the most elegant tree that has ever been introduced into Europe."

In size small, but in material and scope compendious, was *The Gardener's and Planter's Calendar* published in London in 1773 for Richard Weston. The second of several editions, corrected and enlarged, appeared in 1778 and contained "The Method of Raising Timber-Trees, Fruit-Trees, and Quick, for Hedges. With Directions for Forming and Managing A Garden, in Every Month of the Year, Also, many New Improvements in the Art of Gardening To which is added, An Appendix, containing A General Catalogue of Seeds and Plants for the Kitchen-Garden, Flower-Garden, &c."

According to Weston, this work was for those who love the country and "who can have nothing to do with such elegant and expensive amusements" as greenhouses and stoves.

The element of controversy that crept into the garden affairs of the latter part of the eighteenth century is further illustrated in the reflections cast upon other "Gardener's Calendars" by Weston, for which people "pay two or three shillings extraordinary for instructions they have no manner of occasion for." He gives them all they want, he confidently states; "a few plain directions with regard to the proper time and method of raising the necessary vegetables for the table; with some flowers and shrubs for amusement; and, perhaps, some of the common and useful Timber-trees, Fruit-trees and Quicks for repairing the hedges." Unwanted and incomprehensible instructions have been instrumental in the public's foregoing "the most useful and entertaining branches of gardening and planting" or using unimproved methods resulting in slower and shorter returns.

"It is to remedy these evils I have undertaken this small Tract, entirely founded on my own experience, and calculated for the use of those who have but small quantities of land or chuse to confine themselves to the most easy rural operations: such as no person, possessed of even a half an acre, should be ignorant of; especially, the raising of Timber-trees, the easiest of all the rural operations; for, it may be truly affirmed, that an Oak or an Elm may be obtained with much less trouble and expense than a Carnation, a Cucumber, or a Cauliflower."

Weston's book must have been of value to the people of his time for hardly any detail has been overlooked that needs attention during any particular month. How to lay out the land, what kinds of tools are needed for a nursery, and directions for preparing the ground are but a few of the hundreds of instructions to gardeners in this worthy volume.

William Gilpin (1724-1804), who has been touched upon in an earlier chapter by reason of his interest in landscape gardens and his three essays on the picturesque, brought out a work in two volumes appearing in 1791, which do not come under a strictly scientific or practical heading but were the outcome of observations made while traversing the whole of New-Forest. Knowing little of the inhabitants of the forest, everything caught his attention. His notes, jotted in a memorandum book which he always carried with him and placed temporarily under one of two general headings, "Forest Scenery in General" and "The Scenery of Particular Places" finally appeared as *Remarks on Forest Scenery, and other Woodland Views (relative chiefly to Picturesque Beauty)* which the author himself illustrated in mezzotints with scenes of New-Forest in Hampshire. In his dedication to William Mitford, "one of the Verderors of New-Forest," he describes the growth of the work: "Thus as small things lead to greater, an evening walk, or ride, became the foundation of a volume," and to William Mitford he reflects further: "You are as fond of these amusements as I am; and when we trifle, we like to have the sanction of those we esteem to trifle with us...."

As a record of close observation the work is valuable and worthwhile although it lacks the scientific organization of a Linnaeus. In the first of the three books which compose the two volumes, he considers trees as "Single Objects," investigating their general picturesque qualities, in their several kinds and in the specific character of each, "concluding the book with a short account of the most celebrated trees, which have been noticed." The second book

FLORALIA *Worthy Volumes about Trees*

considers "trees under their various modes of *composition* ... under the several picturesque circumstances of *permanent* or *accidental* beauty. ..." The third book is devoted to New-Forest. In his remarks on forest scenery, Gilpin adheres to his belief that trees are the foundation of all scenery.

The books described above are the work of the practical worker and the lover of picturesque nature. One who was out of the gardening world but whose love of botany and trees led him to compile a work wherein detailed descriptions of the characteristics and one might say the personalities of trees are found, was Edward Kennion (1743-1809). Although the work was issued after his death which took place in the early part of the next century, as early as 1779 plans for the work were under way, and from 1782-1789 he was "occupied in the pursuits most congenial to his mind, the study of botany, the improvement of his art, and the collection of materials for his intended work, the Elements of Landscape...."

Kennion's *An Essay on Trees in Landscape: or, an Attempt to Shew the Propriety and Importance of Characteristic Expression in this Branch of Art, and the Means of Producing It: with Examples* contains over fifty plates both as sources of instruction and imitation for the artist and also of interest to the less scientific student of botany. "The Oak, Elm, and Ash, are very fully exhibited in twenty Plates, and thirty more Plates are devoted to the other tenants of our forests and plantations, the whole comprising twenty-four Species and Varieties, and including all

FLORALIA *Worthy Volumes about Trees*

the principal Forest Trees which are found in Great Britain."

During the first of two trips made to Jamaica at the age of nineteen, Kennion commenced the study of botany. On a tour in 1767, he probably felt the first inclination for his art, but that he had paid particular attention to the delineation of trees, appears from some sketches taken in Jamaica, in which the Cocoa, Date, and Banana trees are touched with great delicacy and truth. "As an Artist, Mr. Kennion's chief merit undoubtedly was a close observation and exact imitation of Nature. In Trees this work will suffice to shew how carefully he had studied and how faithfully he had copied her." The editor of the book states further, "It was his leading principle, that Nature, and Nature only, was to be exhibited . . . that truth of representation was never to be violated for the sake of effect."

Kennion criticised the general tendency among artists to depict a tree without showing its distinct character, and gives as example, ". . . an Ash and an Elm are depicted under the same general scrawl called a tree . . ." He observes also, "Yet important as trees are in the composition of landscape, there is nothing in the representation of which Artists more frequently fail." And as an illustration: "Of the several methods in use to manufacture trees, that of representing them by a multitude of *dots* is the worst, and shows the most entire ignorance of nature."

To Kennion, the art of picturing beautiful trees is new. This work, though by an artist to whom a tree was not so much an object for scientific classification as a thing of beauty with a character of its own worthy of transfer to paper, is a valuable representation and depiction of twenty-two different types of trees.

One of the earliest and one of the most important of the eighteenth century books about trees was concerned with America. As early as 1737, Mark Catesby wrote *Hortus Britanno-Americanus or, A Curious Collection of Trees and Shrubs the Produce of the British Colonies in North America; Adopted to The Soil and Climate of England with Observations on Their Constitution, Growth, and Culture: and Directions how they are to be collected, packed up, and secured during their Passage Embellished with Copper plates neatly engraved.* This was first printed in London and came out again in 1763 in a later edition.

The preface begins: "It will be easily imagined that ... the territory of the crown of Great Britain on the continent of America must afford a plentiful variety of trees and shrubs that may be usefully employed to enrich and adorn our woods by their valuable timber and delightful shade; or to embellish and perfume our gardens with the elegance of their appearance and the fragrance of their odours; in both which respects they greatly excel our home productions of the like kind. . . . Nor indeed was an considerable step taken towards introducing these strangers into England till about the year 1729, since which time and through the laudable application of a few persons only, many kinds of American plants, and particularly of forest-trees and shrubs, have been procured and raised from thence; ... By long acquaintance with the trees and shrubs of America, and a constant attention since for several years to their cultivation here, I have been enabled to make such observations on their constitution, growth, and culture, as may render the management of them easy to those who shall be desirous to enrich their country, and give pleasure to themselves, by planting and increasing these beautiful exoticks. Few people have opportunities of procuring these things from America; ... it seems proper to mention, that Mr. Gray at Fulham has for many years made it his business to raise and cultivate the plants of America ... and that through his industry and skill a greater variety of American forest-trees and shrubs may be seen in his gardens than in any other place in England." Catesby says he treats of eighty-five trees and shrubs, sixty-three of which were "graved" and the remaining twenty-two are described, but not "graved" ... "As this small tract is designed entirely for use, I have endeavored to contrive it in the most intelligible and compendious manner I was able."

The first tree described in this volume is the *Magnolia altissima* or the laurel tree of Carolina, of which he says: "Of all the trees able to endure our climate, that have yet been introduced to England, there is none that can equal this magnificent ever-green." Several varieties of oaks are listed, for the "soil and climate of England being so peculiarly adapted to the growth of the oak, it may be reasonably expected that the various species of this tree which America abounds with, should also agree and prosper with us."

FLORALIA *Worthy Volumes about Trees*

A note about the dahoon holly is quite interesting. "This plant is not common in Carolina; it grows particularly at Colonel Bull's plantation on Ashley River, in a bog much frequented by alligators." Following this appears a note about the yapon saying: "In South Carolina it is called Cassena, in Virginia and North Carolina it is known by the name of Yapon." The 30th section describes the sassafras tree which "grows in most parts of North America; its medicinal virtue is very well known as a sweetener of the blood... in Virginia a strong decoction of the root has some times been given with good success for an intermitting fever." The acacia with rose-colored flowers he says is a "rare tree which has lately been procured by Sir John Colliton, Bart. from his plantation at Carolina, and flourishes annually in his gardens at Exmouth in Devonshire."

The next to the last tree described is the palmetto of Carolina. The concluding sentence is: "Sir Hans Sloane observes, that the name of Palm seems best to agree with this kind, because the leaf resembles a hand more than any of the other sorts." The engravings are bound together and follow the descriptive notes. There are four engravings to a page with the exception of the magnolia and the palm trees, to each of which a whole page is devoted.

What is believed to be "the first strictly American botanical work, that is to say, the first treatise on American plants, written by a native American, and printed in this country" appeared in 1785 when Humphry Marshall

FLORALIA *Worthy Volumes about Trees*

(1722-1801) of Chester County, Pennsylvania, published his *Arbustrum Americanum*.

Marshall was the eighth of nine children. Like other children of early settlers, as soon as possible he was put to work around the home. He received only the rudiments of plainest English education and was employed in agricultural labors until he was old enough to be apprenticed to a stonemason. That he was an excellent workman is evident from the walls of his residence at Marshallton built by his own hands.

About the time of his marriage in 1748 he seems to have turned his attention to the acquisition of knowledge, "evincing a decided partiality for Astronomy and Natural History." It is possible that his taste for horticulture and botany was "awakened and promoted by a familiar intercourse with his cousin John Bartram and by the attractions of that cousin's interesting garden." In 1764, he erected a greenhouse, doubtless the first of its kind ever seen or thought of in the county of Chester. Following Bartram's example, he planned and commenced the botanic garden at Marshallton in 1773 and this was "the recipient of the most interesting trees and shrubs of our country, together with many curious exotics."

He was much engaged in collecting native plants and seeds and sending them to Europe. In addition to this interest and activity in horticulture, he indulged his fondness for astronomical observations in a little observatory he constructed in his home. He also spent a well rounded life, for like his father, from whom he inherited the estate in 1767, he was an exemplary and influential member of the Society of Friends. Marshall was active, too, in public affairs, not shirking the responsibilities and duties of public office. Although in later years his vision was greatly impaired, his sight was never entirely lost and he "could discern the walks in his garden, examine his trees and recognize localities of his favourite plants."

The *Arbustrum Americanum,* first begun in 1780, and printed in 1785, is, for that day, a "useful and highly creditable performance." Although its convenience was impaired by the alphabetical arrangement under generic name, the descriptions, in accordance with the Linnaean system are "faithful and satisfactory." The full title of the work was *ARBUSTRUM AMERICANUM: The American Grove or, an Alphabetical Catalogue of Forest Trees and Shrubs, natives of the American United States, arranged according to the Linnaean System, Containing, the particular distinguishing Characters of each Genus with plain, simple and familiar Descriptions of the Manner of Growth, Appearance, &c. of their several Species and Varieties. also, some Hints of their uses in Medicine, Dyes and Domestic Oeconomy.* [COMPILED FROM ACTUAL KNOWLEDGE AND OBSERVATION, AND THE ASSISTANCE OF BOTANICAL AUTHORS.]

Certain of the species not found in Linnaeus's *Species Plantarum* are taken from a sheet catalogue published by John and William Bartram; examples of these are *Franklinea alatahama,* and the Ogeche lime tree of which Marshall says: "This is a tree of great singularity and beauty;

growing naturally in water, in the southern states, and rising to the height of about 30 feet." He adds that this is perhaps the *multiflora* of Weston.

In Marshall's introduction to the book he states ". . . the science of Botany, or that branch . . . which teaches the right knowledge of Vegetables, and their application to the most beneficial uses . . . merits the attention and encouragement of every patriotic and liberal mind as among the first of useful pursuits." He felt that it was particularly important to the members of the commonwealth, for considering the "continual enormous expence we are at in purchasing foreign Teas, Drugs, Dye stuffs &c." the country should make a special effort to reduce this cost and he advocated two important steps.

The first of these steps was "The introduction and cultivation of foreign useful and valuable plants" and this he felt was possible by the extent of territory, diversity of climate, soil and situation of his country. Marshall recommended the growing of the tea plant because the purchase of this commodity was "one of the greatest drains of our wealth." This he thought might thrive well in Southern States. "In this same view the Vine, the Almond Tree, the Fig Tree, Licorice, Madder and Rhubarb, deservedly require our attention." The second step should be "The discovering the qualities and uses of our own Native Vegetable production, and applying them to the most useful purposes . . . Our being able to discover a plant of equal general usage to the potatoe, tobacco, or ginseng, for example, or a good substitute for Tea, Coffee and Peruvian

FLORALIA *Worthy Volumes about Trees*

Bark would be advantages surpassing all adequate estimation."

For all this is needed a knowledge of botany and thus the author to "tender a knowledge of this subject more familiar and easy has been induced to draw up his alphabetical Catalogue of the Forest trees and shrubs, natives of the American United States as mentioned in the best authors or since discovered by ingenious travellers."

To use Marshall's own words, the entire book, written in plain and familiar language since "the generality of his Readers would have been more embarrassed and confused than profited" from a work full of notes of reference and synonyms, forms a useful and practical "Botanical Companion."

The next work devoted to American trees was published in Göttingen in 1781 by Friedrich Adam Julius von Wangenheim, and was entitled *Beschreibung einiger nordamerikanischen Holz- und Buscharten* describing certain of the forest trees found in America. Von Wangenheim (1747-1800) was a Hessian officer in the employ of the King of England who fought in the war of the revolution. In the pauses of the conflict he found opportunity to study the trees of the colonies with reference to their value for introduction into the forests of Germany. His book, illustrated with thirty-one pages and seventy-two rude figures, describes one hundred and sixty-eight trees and shrubs, all of which are classified according to the systems of Linnaeus and Gronovius, and has at the end an index in German and English. The list of trees touched upon by him is notable more for its wide variety than for intensity, for only three kinds of oaks are included.

In 1758, in France a valuable two-volume work by Duhamel du Monceau appeared entitled *La Physique des Arbres: où il est Traité de l'Anatomie des Plantes et de l'Economie Végétale.*

The author of this work, a member of the Royal Academy of Sciences, the Royal Society of London, and other honorary institutions, provided in his work an introduction to a complete treatise on woods and trees and included a dissertation on the methods of botany.

The book contains an interesting preface, followed by an outline of the work in botanical classification which preceded the eighteenth century. Following that, he gives an outline of each of the systems of Morrison, Ray, Tournefort, Magnol, and Linnaeus. The five books which compose the two volumes cover, in the first book, the anatomy of trees; in the second, the buds, flowers and fruits; in the third, the organs of fructification and the use of the different parts; in the fourth, such topics as the seeds, their germination and the growth of the tree; in the fifth, among other items, the diseases of trees and what remedies can be applied. It is a highly valuable and scientifically written work, and contains many detailed illustrations and diagrams.

A most important work about American trees, written by André Michaux, appeared, as already mentioned, in 1801, *L'Histoire des Chênes de l'Amérique,* in which was a description of the species and varieties of oaks found in

America. During his residence on this continent, Michaux, "in order to satisfy himself, and clear up his doubts, sowed and cultivated during his residence . . . all the species he observed and collected; and on the second year, he had the satisfaction to discover all the varieties, which had occasioned him so many uncertainties, when he wandered over the forests." He discovered in the very young trees, by carefully observing the changes assumed by certain kinds, the characteristic marks of their species; thus he obtained a knowledge of the relations which arise among them.

After attempting to obtain distinguishing characteristics based on the parts of fructification and the structure of the cup of the acorn, he then made observations on the leaves which afforded him more striking characteristics and these he has used in order to establish two sections of oaks. "The first section contains such species as have awnless leaves, or in other words, which have no bristly points; the second, those with leaves, whose points or indentations are terminated by a bristle or an awn." The secondary characteristics he established are based on the interval of time between the appearance of the flower and the ripening of the fruit with two secondary divisions arising out of annual fructification and biennial fructification.

Michaux's work on oaks, illustrated by Pierre Joseph Redouté in black and white engravings, is divided into twenty sections, under the two groupings. It is a scholarly work, giving classification numbers according to the systems of Linnaeus, Gronovius, Kalm, Miller's *Dictionary*, and others and contains an interesting bibliography showing that he was well versed in the work of his contemporaries, for in addition to the above mentioned names, Aiton, Bartram, Walter, Marshall, Van Wangenheim, and Duhamel are spoken of among others. The characteristics of each species are considered in logical outline order under the headings of the height, the bark, the leaves, fructification, place found, and general observations. In all, it is a most valuable work.

CHAPTER VII

William Curtis: The Founder of the Botanical Magazine

"THE SEASON OF THE YEAR seems now to invite you to the pursuit of botany; a science which, if not essentially necessary to you in the line of any particular profession, it is at least deserving some share of your attention as men, as rational beings."

Thus began the first of William Curtis's *Lectures on Botany*. This opening paragraph is indicative of the man and the work which he wished to do for the world. To him botany was so vitally tied up with the welfare of mankind, that any one could ill afford to be entirely ignorant of it. Although tremendous progress in the natural sciences had been made since the beginning of the century, he realized that there was still a profound lack of botanical knowledge among the populace in general and the medical profession in particular. He attributed this "inattention," as he called it, to a want of opportunity to acquire it, and he felt that if some means were provided for studying botany, there would no longer be cause for complaint or censure. He was not the first to sense this need, for early in the century Dr.

FLORALIA *William Curtis*

William Sherard had founded a botanical professorship at Oxford. John James Dillenius, as has been noted in a foregoing chapter, was appointed to the position, and while he successfully supervised the garden he was a failure as a professor. Dr. Sibthorp, who held the post for the next forty years, was scarcely more active than his predecessor had been. So it is not to be wondered at that Curtis was impatient about the ineffective method of disseminating botanical knowledge. His whole life was an expression of effort to give to the world enlightenment in this particular branch of science.

From boyhood through early manhood William Curtis had a struggle with the world in a profession that he did not like. In 1760, when fourteen years of age, much against his wishes, he was apprenticed to his grandfather, an apothecary at Alton, to learn the arts and mysteries of the medical profession. Coincident with his lessons in medicine he came into his first lessons in botany. Curtis formed a friendship with John Legg, the ostler at the Crown Inn, which was close by his grandfather's house. The ostler, though an unlettered man, had gained by his own efforts a complete knowledge of plants from the volumes of Gerard and Parkinson, and this he passed on to his young pupil. A remarkable friendship, coming as it did during young Curtis's impressionable years, set in motion powers that eventually made him famous. Under Legg's guidance and with the help of Berkenhout's botanical lexicon, Curtis knew in a short time all of the wild plants in the neighborhood. By the time his apprenticeship came to a close, he had a very excellent knowledge of the plants which related to medicine.

It was probably with great relief that Curtis shook loose the fetters that had bound him to his family. When he was exactly twenty years old he went up to London to complete his medical studies. At first he lived with Mr. George Vaux, surgeon in Pudding Lane, and afterward with Mr. Thomas Talwin, apothecary of Grace Church Street, to whose practice he finally fell heir.

The next few years were very important ones in the development of Curtis's career as a botanist. At St. Thomas's Hospital he attended anatomical lectures given by Mr. Else and Dr. Fordyce, and fortunately these two men held the thought in common with him that botanical knowledge was necessary to the education of medical students. He early believed what he later expressed: "That the Benevolent Author of Nature has given to each country plants proper for the care of diseases peculiar to its inhabitants, and many good reasons may be brought in support of that opinion." Because of the knowledge that he had acquired before coming to London, Curtis proved himself so valuable in these classes that he was made botanical assistant to the lecturers. While he kept this appointment he would take his pupils into the fields and woods around London not only to study botany, for he connected with it the study of entomology. This whole experience as assistant to his instructors, as well as his field work, in a very large way determined his future accomplishments as a botanist. His boyish attempts to learn

William Curtis

FLORALIA *William Curtis*

about the plants and insects around his home would have met with frustration had it not been for his ostler friend. Now for the first time, his love for natural history was not only sanctioned but encouraged by his superiors. The feeling that his great interest in every branch of this subject was in accordance with medical research gave him a sense of satisfaction and assurance of its real worth. The desire that had long been taking form within him, that as soon as it was expedient he would give up his medical work which he carried on because of necessity and not from choice, and would devote his entire time to natural science, crystallized into a determination. His first step in this direction was to take on a partner, Mr. Wavell, whose help prevented the practice from collapsing altogether. However, it was said that this young man was "of the same turn of mind as Mr. Curtis, though less ardent, and they were engaged in the same pursuits at all leisure opportunities." Perhaps it was just as well for the patients concerned that Mr. Curtis soon gave up the practice of medicine altogether.

The thought was always strong within him which he voiced in one of his botanical lectures: "Providence in his unerring wisdom having allotted to mankind different capacities and implanted in them propensities to particular pursuits, so that what is a matter of greatest satisfaction to one, should be perfectly insipid to another." Believing in his own propensities and working toward that end, William Curtis arrived when scarcely more than thirty years old at a place where he was "unfettered and left to the bias of his own mind." His declaration of freedom was the purchase of a piece of land in Grange Road, Bermondsey, where he began his first botanic garden. Thomas White, the brother of the famous Selborne naturalist, Reverend Gilbert White, was associated with him in this work.

Mr. Curtis apparently had a great capacity for friendship, and his activities had caused him to "become known to many gentlemen of the first abilities in the knowledge of natural history." One of these, Mr. Alchorne, recommended him "in the handsomest terms as Demonstrator of Botany and Proefectus Horti to the Society of Apothecaries," to which position he was appointed, and which he held for many years. Curtis was enthusiastic in accepting the appointment and though it was "always more honourable than lucrative," he felt that it was an opportunity for the advancement of scientific knowledge of plants. "What a heartfelt satisfaction," he said, "must attend the person who should discover a specific for cancer, or any other dreadful disease. It were to be wished that the faculty were as eager after discoveries of this kind as chemists were formerly in search after the philosopher's stone. The prospect of success is perhaps more promising, the attempt at least is much more laudable."

Curtis had reason to be convinced of the fundamental importance of the work that he was doing. The knowledge came to him that in certain sections of the country some medical men were making extracts from cow parsley instead of from hemlock, and he remarked feelingly, "It is

FLORALIA *William Curtis*

much to be feared that mistakes of this sort frequently frustrate the well-meant endeavours of the physician." He felt that to be acquainted with the medicinal character of English plants was the duty of every one who assumed the responsibility as guardian of the health of mankind. He gave a most enlightening example of what could happen to a person who was misguided in his knowledge of medicinal plants when he told of the dire results that followed the eating of a handful of fool's parsley by a publican of the town. He felt that the physicians too often depended upon the ignorant and illiterate for many of "their efficacious officinal plants, frequently at the expense of their own characters and all that was valuable to their patients."

In the meantime the Grange Road Garden proved itself too small for Mr. Curtis's plans and he then bought a place in Lambeth Marsh where he gathered the largest collection of British plants ever brought together in one place. Sir Joseph Banks and other eminent botanists and scientists of that day not only encouraged him in this establishment of a regular school for studying plants from nature but made annual contribution to carry on the work. Many wonderful gifts of plants were received for this garden; some came from "His Majesty's matchless collection in the Royal Garden at Kew." Curtis divided his plants into four groups, medicinal, culinary, common poisoners, and British, and planted them in the four equal divisions of his garden. Then he worked out and published catalogues of his garden that were amusing as well as instructive. Seven editions of the catalogue of this garden were published, the first of which appeared in 1783. This carried a description of more than six thousand plants. However, for all of the thought and planning and work that was done for this garden, the location proved unfavorable. Smoke stifled many of the small plants, and the soil was unsuitable to others. Still strong in his determination to have a garden, he bought some land at Brompton on the outskirts of London. The garden proper occupied three and one half acres and there were seven acres adjoining for sea kale and experimental agricultural crops. He laid out his new garden and then moved the plants from Lambeth Marsh into it. His active mind was continually making plans for additions to the collection which he considered deficient, and he made journeys to different parts of the country and brought back many excellent finds. His hopes and expectations were reasonably justified in the Brompton gardens and here he lived and worked for the rest of his life.

The purpose which was always uppermost in Mr. Curtis's mind was to apply science in such a way that mankind would be benefited. He said: "It is not to physic alone that botany is subservient; perhaps it is applied with as much advantage to agriculture, which is extremely defective .... and the improvement of which is the only solid check to the baneful and enervating effects of luxury and dissipations." In his book on British grasses he wrote very feelingly on the need of the application of more scientific knowledge to agriculture. He struck at the core of the

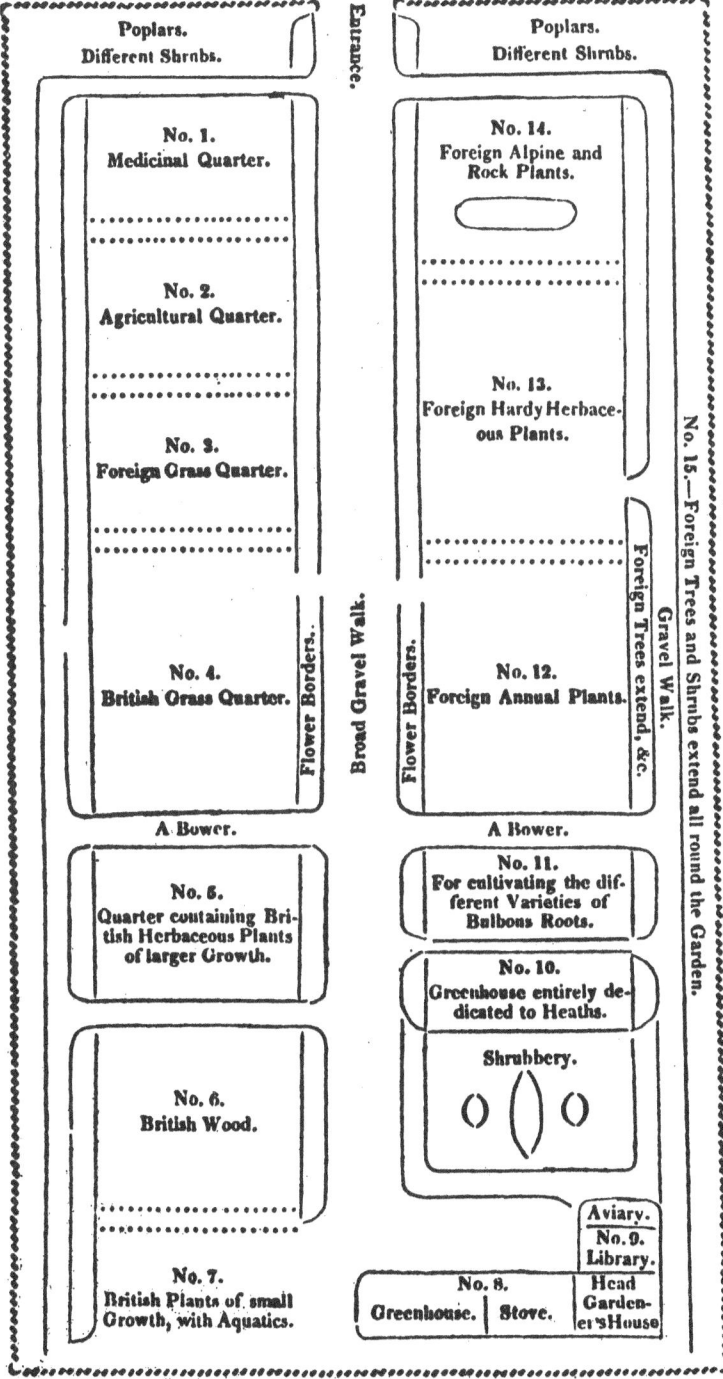

trouble when he said: "Improvements in any science, but more especially in agriculture, are slow in their advances; and, perhaps, no class of men adheres more pertinaciously to old prejudices than the farmer."

Feeling that much of the meadow and pasture land of England was capable of greater production, Curtis made a study of the grasses. Out of one hundred and three species that grew, only one was cultivated for pasturage and that was deficient in many requisites of a good grass. Curtis cultivated small plots of many varieties. In 1787 he published *Practical Observations on the British Grasses,* in which he made recommendations as a result of his observations and experiments. He wrote: "The grasses recommended will, I am confident, do all that our natural grasses can do. There are six of those which should constitute the bulk of our best pastures." These were: sweet vernal, meadow foxtail, smooth stalk meadow, rough stalk meadow, meadow fescue, crested foxtail. There are six uncolored plates in the book, illustrating the six grasses. And the author concludes by saying: "But let no one expect these to perform wonders, for after all they are but grasses, and, as such, are liable to produce great or small crops, according to particular seasons, or to the fertility or barrenness of the soil on which they are grown." This valuable pamphlet was highly effective in improving this particular phase of agriculture.

Another contribution which Mr. Curtis made was the introduction of the *Crambe maritima* or sea kale as a culinary vegetable. He wrote a pamphlet which told of its attributes and how to grow it, and this accompanied each box of seed sold in order that its cultivation might be expedited.

For all of Curtis's extensive knowledge, his experimentations and his explorations into tangible and intangible fields, his writings that have come down to posterity are comparatively few. Although they show an individual and amusing style, he felt that his training had been very deficient. Perhaps that and a natural modesty accounted for a limited output of literary productions. In his memoirs left to a friend he said: "I have no pretensions to be considered as a man of letters, or of great mental powers. A consciousness of my inabilities makes me diffident, and produces in me a shyness, which some have been ready to construe into pride." Curtis's first publication was a pamphlet, *Instructions for Collecting and Preserving Insects*. This appeared in 1771 at the time that he was botanical assistant to his anatomy professors during his early days in London. This and a lecture on insects which is bound with his lectures on botany are among the very few of his writings on entomology which have been preserved. He wrote two other pamphlets which were the results of his observations as botanical assistant. One was *Wild Plants in the Environs of London,* in 1774, and the other he wrote in 1776, which was called *Fructification of Mosses*. Curtis early realized that one of the reasons botany was little better understood by people in general in England in the 1770's was because all of the material on the subject was so unorganized and there was no existing list of plants commonly used. He communicated with all of the botanists and scientists in England and on the Continent, and every bit of useful information that he gathered he put into methodical order. Then in 1771 he translated and published his *Fundamenta Entomologiae* of Linnaeus. Feeling that there was need for further work in this field, he brought out in 1777 *Linnaeus's system of Botany, so far as relates to his Classes and Orders of Plants, Illustrated by figures*—"Entirely new with Copious Explanatory Descriptions." This was dedicated to John Gideon Loten, Esq., formerly Governor of the Islands, Ceylon and Celebes. Most likely this gentleman was a contributor of rare plants to the botanic gardens. In the preface of the book Curtis says: "Among the various systems of Botany none appears to have been so universally received or so likely to continue to future generations as that of the great, celebrated Linnaeus, and had the drawings which have been given to illustrate it been equal to the author's descriptions, it would doubtless have made a more rapid progress and had been more generally and perfectly understood than it is at present. With respect to the orders, the attempt of exhibiting them at one view is, so far as I know, altogether novel. If proper attention be paid to the figures and explanations here, I flatter myself, a knowledge of the classes and orders will readily be acquired, and the student having overcome what has been a stumbling block to many, will be tempted to make further progress in this useful and delightful science, in which I wish him much pleasure and improvement." The plates were designed by Sowerby and

FLORALIA *William Curtis*

engraved by Sansom. Some of them were exquisitely colored, while others were uncolored.

Soon after Curtis established his first garden in Bermondsey, he conceived the idea of beginning the publication of the folio, *Flora Londinensis*, which has become his greatest work. This stretched over a period of years from 1775-1798. The title-page is self-explanatory:

Flora Londinensis
or
Plates and Descriptions of Such Plants as Grow Wild
in the environs of London
with
Their Places of Growth, and Time of Flowering; their several names according to Linnaeus and other authors—
with a particular description of each plant in Latin
and English
To which are added their several uses in Medicine, Agriculture, Rural Oeconomy, and other Arts.

The parts were issued at uncertain intervals and sometimes these intervals were very wide apart. While this was an advantage in point of accuracy, it was a disadvantage as far as sales were concerned. Many investigations have been made to discover the order in which the plates to *Flora Londinensis* appeared, but apparently the efforts have met with little success. The work contains six fasciculi, sometimes bound in two volumes and sometimes in three. Each fasciculus has seventy-two plates. These were originally issued in numbers; each number containing six plates, making a total of four hundred and thirty-two plates. But neither the parts nor plates were numbered until 101 was reached. The plates were done by some of the foremost artists of the times. It has been suggested that some of the figures which do not carry signatures were probably done by Mr. Curtis himself. William Kilburn, who lived in the neighborhood, did some of the early numbers. Mr. Milton, a noted engraver, helped at times, and James Sowerby and Mr. F. Sansom made many contributions. However, the person who was of most value to Mr. Curtis, not only as artist, but also as counselor and companion as well, was Sydenham Taste Edwards. When a very young man he was employed by Mr. Curtis, who discovered his remarkable talent, and, afterwards sent him to London for further training. Edwards drew and etched the plates for practically all of Mr. Curtis's later work. Mr. Curtis, though self-taught, was an adept at engraving and drawing. One of his contemporaries said of him: "His eye was truly microscopic; nothing escaped his remark and his discernment was most critical. His descriptions of plants are, therefore, perfect. He could direct the artist to express what he himself felt. And if ever he suffered his mind to be ruffled, it was when the painter had not fulfilled his part exactly to his mind."

The publication of *Flora Londinensis* with its excellent descriptions and beautiful illustrations brought universal admiration and established the reputation of Curtis as a foremost botanist. Because of the cost of production and the slowness of its appearance, it never paid expenses.

FLORALIA *William Curtis*

The sale of copies did not exceed three hundred. Mr. Curtis was much disturbed when a fellow member of the Linnaean Society, Dr. Smith, started the publication of a work which he called *English Botany;* this was illustrated by James Sowerby who had done some of the plates for *Flora Londinensis*. Mr. Curtis took the publication of this work as a personal insult and for a time he severed his connection with the Linnaean Society, of which he had been a charter member. However, he thought better of it. Perhaps Dr. Thornton's observation, that the *English Botany* left Mr. Curtis's work to shine with undiminished splendor, had its effect.

If *Flora Londinensis* brought no financial return, the *Botanical Magazine or Flower Garden Displayed* more than compensated for this. The first volume of the magazine appeared in 1787 under the title:

The Botanical Magazine
or
Flower Garden Displayed
in which
The most ornamental Foreign plants cultivated
in the Open Ground, the Green-House, and the
stove will be accurately represented in
their Natural Colours, to which
will be added their Names, Class, Order
Generic and Specific Characters according to
the celebrated Linnaeus; their places of growth,
and Times of Flowering. London 1787.

FLORALIA *William Curtis*

In speaking of his two most important publications, Mr. Curtis said: "One brought me pudding and the other brought me praise." From its very beginning to the day of the author's death, July 7, 1799, this magazine brought him an income on which he could live and carry on his scientific investigations with much ease. The idea of such a work was new, but the time was ripe for its appearance and it filled a real need. It met with the approval of not only the scientists of the time but the laity as well. The magazine came out in monthly numbers, each number containing three plates with descriptions which corresponded to the plates. The monthly sale was about two thousand copies. This journal has appeared continuously and is published today by the Royal Horticultural Society of London.

Mr. Curtis maintained for the *Botanical Magazine* a very high type of illustration. The majority of plates for the thirteen volumes which he edited were done by his close associate, Sydenham T. Edwards. James Sowerby, who later became the illustrator for *English Botany,* and F. Sansom also did many of the plates. Sometimes they combined their talents; many of the plates were designed by Edwards and engraved by Sansom. There has been much discussion and speculation about the unsigned plates in these early numbers of the magazine. The general impression has been that they were done by Curtis himself. However, there are some critics who attribute them to Edwards, while an article in the *Gardener's Chronicle* suggests that they might have been done by a very excellent but little known artist, Philippa Crabtree, who did very accurate and beautiful botanical drawings during the latter part of the eighteenth century.

The *Lectures on Botany*, which were given over a long period and to varied groups, were not published until after Mr. Curtis's death in 1799. Ultimately, these lectures were edited and published in 1803-04 by Samuel Curtis, a cousin, who had married William Curtis's adopted daughter. Much of the spirit of the lectures as given by the author was lost because notes in shorthand which interlined the manuscript could not be used.

William Curtis's accomplishments for the numbers of years that he lived were tremendous. Loving botany from the very beginning of his life, he became, largely by his own efforts, the first real teacher of that science in his country, as well as the founder of the first magazine on the subject.

CHAPTER VIII

Pierre Joseph Redouté: The Raphael of Flowers

THE ART OF COLOR PRINTING at the beginning of the eighteenth century received a tremendous impetus from the introduction of new methods of engraving. Etchings, mezzotints, aquatints, as well as line engravings, antedated this period, although they had not been widely used. In 1680 Johannes Tyler in Holland made the discovery that it was possible to paint a copper plate in colored inks in such manner as to produce in one printing a colored picture. Early in the century James Christopher Le Blon, who stands out as an important figure in the artistic circles of his age, invented his three-color process in the production of mezzotints and this important achievement, on the heels of the Tyler discovery, more or less unloosed the shackles which had heretofore held color printing within narrow limits. With Bartolozzi as the guiding genius, colored printing and engraving joined hands in stipple engraving, and from this there resulted an important decorative movement.

Floral illustration during the eighteenth century at-

FLORALIA *Pierre Joseph Redouté*

tained a peak of near perfection that had never before been reached; there were artists who expressed themselves in this field of illustration beautifully and almost perfectly. The spirit and genius which characterized illustration of the time did not slow down at the end of the century, and the impetus was sufficient to carry it over. Some of the illustrators who claimed the eighteenth century for theirs by right of birth continued to do beautiful work during the first quarter of the century that followed. One of these was Pierre Joseph Redouté who was born on the tenth of July, 1759, at St. Hubert, a small town in the picturesque district of Ardennes near Liége.

Redouté, whom his contemporaries called the Raphael of Flowers, stands out among the celebrated artists of his time. He influenced all flower painting, and colored floral illustration will forever be associated with his name. While John James Audubon painted the birds of America, Redouté painted the flowers of France, and these two great artists of Nature, who lived and created during the same period, each, in his chosen specialty, achieved a level that has never been equalled, and time only will tell if they will ever be excelled. Again like Audubon, Redouté had little formal instruction in art. He learned from his father the principles of design, and from then on he had no other teachers but his own genius and nature. His talent, born with him, seemed, like the man, never to have had a period of infancy.

As the son, grandson, and great-grandson of Belgian ecclesiastical painters, who more or less spent their lives

FLORALIA *Pierre Joseph Redouté*

decorating and painting the interior of churches, it is natural that young Redouté should have devoted his first efforts to the adornment of the churches of his country. At thirteen years of age, he left his family, and taking nothing with him for his fortune but his palette, brushes and a strong wish to excel in his art, went from village to village studying the masterpieces of ancient Flanders and Holland. He wanted to understand the freedom in tone and the delicate touch which characterized the two schools. He spent a year at Vilvorde where he painted the designs of doors and did decorations and pictures in churches. He became so well known in the course of his wanderings that by the time he was sixteen years old he was asked by the painter, André, to help decorate the Château de Calsbourg near Bouillon.

In 1776 he traveled again in Flanders, and in the course of this trip, the wonderful floral pictures of the great Van Huysum were brought to his attention. These made such a profound impression on his mind and so fascinated him by their beauty, that he then and there decided to make the painting of flowers his life work. He was not, however, to go into this particular phase of art immediately. Through the influence of a friend, the Princess of Tornaco, whom his talent and work had brought him, he was asked to go to Luxembourg to paint portraits of some distinguished persons of that section, among whom was the governor of the province. His patroness then urged him to go to Paris, and she gave him letters of introduction to influential people. Redouté did go to Paris, but he carelessly

FLORALIA *Pierre Joseph Redouté*

lost the letters on the way, no doubt to the impatience of the lady who had written them.

When the young artist reached the city, he had the good fortune to have as his protector and employer an older brother, Antoine-Ferdinand (1756-1809), who had for several years painted and decorated the theaters in Paris with much distinction. Under his tutelage Redouté produced many charming scenes of pastoral life, and by repeatedly bringing forth fresh and lovely creations of this type, he became known as a specialist in this particular field. Scenes depicting shepherds surrounded by flowers in large groves became very popular, so much so in fact, that the epoch of Watteau, that painter of gay fêtes, was revived.

This type of work brought to Redouté the realization that he wanted to paint flowers, not after the chosen manner of ornamental painters, but in making his designs and coloring he wished to give attention to the forms of the plants and their manner of growth. He soon abandoned decorative painting in order to give his time and effort exclusively and wholeheartedly to the study of plants. Here again is found a similarity in the careers of Audubon and Redouté. Each man, after serving an apprenticeship, which did not always provide the necessary bread and butter, arrived at that crisis where he must decide whether or not he would go into an uncertain and untried field where, if he arrived, he would realize the largest and happiest expression of life, in painting the objects he loved most, or whether he would remain at a dead level in comparative security. Both made affirmative decisions, and out of both decisions came remarkable achievements.

Guided by his instinct of genius, Redouté went into the study of the organization of plants. As one studies anatomy in order to understand painting of the human body, this artist dissected plants in order to understand better the painting of flowers. He did not paint by chance, but on the contrary, he made a very serious study of the science of botany, for he wished to penetrate the mysteries of those fascinating and fragile caprices of nature. It was by very careful study that he came to understand the toilette of Flora, and that he became a worthy painter of it. Redouté achieved such astounding success with his painting of flower pictures, that one feels some special secrets were revealed to him. As a medium to express his early efforts he used water colors; they gave a vigor of tone that, somehow, never seemed to be gotten from oil. In 1784 he painted some branches of flowering shrubs and engraved them. By chance these fell into the hands of the botanists, L'Héritier and Gérard Van Spaendonck who, struck by the talent of the artist, influenced him in making his decision to give himself exclusively to this form of illustration.

Redouté designed the figures for the works of L'Héritier, which began a kind of revolution in *l'iconographie botanique*. He accompanied this botanist to London and designed more than five hundred figures of plants for *Sertum Anglicum*. In 1650, by the order of Gaston d'Orléans, a collection of paintings was begun; to this twenty were added each year. When Van Spaendonck, in

FLORALIA *Pierre Joseph Redouté*

the capacity of painter in the cabinet of Louis XVI, invited Redouté to paint rare plants to add to this collection, he set a seal of approval on this artist, which stamped him as a floral painter of achievement.

As the output of his work increased, Redouté's fame as a floral painter spread, and when his work came to the notice of Marie Antoinette, she had him come to Petit Trianon. The Queen loved devotedly the flowers in her parterres which she cultivated with her own hands, and the artist had the good fortune to please her by the way he reproduced them. In this rustic retreat where none of the grandeurs of court life were observed, Redouté, amid royal encouragement, found opportunity to express some of his ambitions. Unfortunately, none of the work of this period was ever shown. During the revolution of 1792, practically all of these paintings, many of them unfinished, were destroyed.

He invented and worked out a new method of stipple engraving and color printing in 1796. When the new regime was established after the revolution, Redouté was given a position in the Museum of Natural History, which carried the title of Master of Design, and here he had opportunity to put into use his own method which he had perfected. He also taught classes in L'École Inconographie des Plantes, where he distinguished himself as teacher as well as artist. Many men and women from all over the world, as well as from every level of society, attended this school, and he numbered among his pupils many distinguished people. In 1805 he received the commission of

FLORALIA *Pierre Joseph Redouté*

Painter of Flowers from Empress Josephine, who, like Marie Antoinette, had a just appreciation of his work. During his long career he was noted as being a favorite of queens. In addition to the two royal ladies already mentioned, he gave lessons to the Duchess de Berry, to Queen Hortense, to Marie Amélie, also to her daughters, Marie and Louise d'Orléans, and to Madame Adelaide, sister of Louis Philippe. He was later recognized by kings as well, for he was given the Legion of Honor from Charles X, a medal from Louis XVIII, as well as L'Ordre de Leopold from the royal family of Belgium.

There was not a flower of the garden, field, or forest that Redouté did not paint faithfully and devotedly. He was solemn and almost speechless in the presence of his models. He knew their names, their perfumes and habits; to him, who was their painter and who held them in genuine affection, they were endowed with immortal spirits. He was happy to see them and paint them *con amore*. Through his intensive study of plants, Redouté became an excellent botanist and an accomplished gardener, as well as a foremost artist.

It is from the numerous books which he illustrated with his new method of color engraving that Redouté became famous. Some volumes he wrote, illustrated and published himself; for others he only supplied the illustrations. The principal ones in this last category are:

La Flora atlantica de Desfontaines. 2 vols. 1798-1800

Le Jardin de la Malmaison par Ventenat. 2 vols. 1803-1804

REDOUTÉ'S DAHLIA

FLORALIA *Pierre Joseph Redouté*

Les Plantes rares du jardin de Cels par Ventenat. 1800

Les Plantes rares du Château de Navarre par A. Bonplaud. 1813

Les Arbres et Arbustes par Duhamel. 7 vols. [1800]-1819

La Botanique de J. J. Rousseau. 1805

Les Plantes grasses d'A. P. Candolle. 1802

La Flora boreali-americana d'And. Michaux. 2 vols. 1803

L'Histoire des Chênes de L'Amériq. d'And. Michaux. 1801

L'Histoire des arbres forestiers de l'Amérique du Nord d'A. F. Michaux fils. 3 vols. 1810-1813

L'Histoire naturelle du Mais de Bonafous. 1 vol. 1836

Among Redouté's own publications were many remarkable works. One of the most beautiful was published under the title of *Les Liliacées*. This came out in eight volumes; the text was written by De Candolle, and it was illustrated with four hundred and eighty-six colored plates. The Empress Josephine and De Chaptal, Minister of the Interior, sponsored the work. This publication was used by the government as an example of the superiority of the products of the French School and in 1804 De Chaptal subscribed for eighty copies which were sent to distinguished artists and scholars throughout Europe. Napoleon, who was always glad to encourage anything which reflected glory on France, instructed Talleyrand, his Minister of Foreign Affairs, to send a number of copies to foreign rulers. There were several editions of *Les Liliacées*. One single copy on vellum made for Josephine was said to have cost 84,000 francs.

The work, however, which gained Redouté the reputation of genius in his chosen field was *Les Roses,* sometimes known as the *Monographie des Roses.* It is considered the most remarkable and most beautiful of all his publications. The first edition appeared during the years from 1817 to 1824, the text of which was written by the botanist, C. A. Thory. It was made up of thirty parts and was published in three volumes by Didot. The first volume begins with the following sentences: "Les poëtes ont fondé dans l'opinion les seules monarchies héréditaires que le temps a respectées: le lion est toujours le roi des animaux, l'aigle, le monarque des airs, et la rose, la reine des fleurs. Les droits des deux premiers, établis sur la force et maintenus par elle, avaient en euxmêmes la raison suffisante de leur durée; la souveraineté de la rose, moins violemment reconnue et plus librement consentie, a quelque chose de plus flatteur pour le trône et de plus honorable pour les fondateurs."

The second edition appeared in large octavo; this was followed in three years by the third edition. *Les Roses de Redouté* were talked of everywhere and they aroused much enthusiasm and admiration.

All kinds of roses are illustrated in these volumes and there is a colored plate for every rose described. Below each plate the name of the rose is in Latin and French and the description by Thory gives quite a detailed account: the height of the bush, the division of the limbs, and the leaves;

FLORALIA *Pierre Joseph Redouté*

it also tells the number of petals in the *observation* where some additional facts are given. The cabbage rose and the *centifolia* are to be found, as well as the York and Lancaster roses. The single roses are very exquisite. There are lovely illustrations of *Le Rosier de Lady Banks*, both yellow and white; this rose was named in honor of the wife of Sir Joseph Banks. All of the prints were delicate and beautiful and the great ladies of the day used these illustrations to decorate their salons and boudoirs. It has been said: "The rose has had her poets, her historians, and now Redouté has become her painter." The accomplishment of the artist in the illustrations of these volumes at the high-water mark of his career was sufficient to substantiate this claim.

Redouté brought out a collection under the title: *Choix des plus belles fleurs prises dans différentes familles du règne végétal*. This work was illustrated with his colored plates, and he dedicated it to the Princesses Louise and Marie d'Orléans. Later he published a volume called *Collection de jolies petites choisies*, and this was followed by *Chois de 60 Roses*. This last was dedicated to another of his royal patronesses, the Queen of the Belgians, who never forgot the artist whom she called *son bon maître*. One volume entitled *Trente dessins originaux de fleurs* was very beautifully made up by the bookmaker, Pilinski Adam, and Redouté did thirty exquisite paintings for it on vellum. The *Album de Redouté* was dedicated to the Duchess de Berry. In this folio volume were brought together twenty-six plates that had been used to illustrate earlier works.

FLORALIA *Pierre Joseph Redouté*

Some of his most beautiful roses and lilies were used in making this album. Excellent work is found in *La Botanique* of J. J. Rousseau; this book is a reprint of Rousseau's *Elementary Letters to a Lady*, to which Redouté added sixty-five colored plates. Perhaps the reason that Redouté did such excellent work in this is that he did it for his own pleasure. The last work of Redouté was a choice collection of his roses, published after his death, under the title, *Bouquet royal*, and dedicated by his widow to the royal family of France.

Other than the books which he illustrated, Redouté did a tremendous number of water colors for the Museum of Natural History. The number has been estimated at more than six thousand. It is claimed that he did equally many in oils. His works were exhibited with great distinction and honor in the salons of 1793, 1804, 1814, 1819, 1822, and 1834. Collections of his original works are rare because large numbers of them were destroyed in the Louvre in the terrible days of 1871.

There was something in Redouté's own process of stipple engraving which gave to his illustrations an indefinable quality which was luminous and almost transparent. Since he was no longer hampered by lines, the artist employed fine shadings which set his illustrations apart and made them different from those of any other engraver. He had the ability to achieve gradations from vivid to soft tones and to create harmony amid a diversity of colors. Aside from the charm and perfection of composition and the beauty of coloring, Redouté's flowers are remarkably exact

FLORALIA *Pierre Joseph Redouté*

botanically. And the hands that created these masterpieces were not the long slender hands that usually belong to the artist, but they were as thick and distorted as those of a day laborer. Redouté mastered his art in such a way that he made it serve him to express his wishes. His fellow artists recognized and accorded him pre-eminence in this chosen specialty of floral painting.

More active and productive years were given to Redouté than are given to most men. At three years of age he began painting and he was actively engaged in this work which he loved so absorbingly until his eighty-first year. Unlike Audubon, he suffered no cessation of his active faculties, but he died of cerebral hemorrhage while giving a lesson to a promising student. Two days later his wife and daughter accompanied by men of letters and artists carried all that was mortal of the great painter to the Cemetery du Pere-La-Chaise. Roses and lilies made into the insignias of the orders by which he had been honored were placed on his grave. Bonafous, a close friend, read a poem which terminated:

> O peintre aimé de Flore et du riant empire!
> Tu nous quittes le jour où le printemps expire!

CHAPTER IX

A Medley of Blossoms

"UNDER THE PATRONAGE of a general taste for their acquisition" exotics came pouring into European gardens from every country and every climate during the entire eighteenth century with England foremost in acclimatizing the newcomers. From early in the century the Society of Gardeners had special interest in this phase of floriculture and from the time Kew Gardens were established the officials in charge aimed to make it a repository of all known plants. William Aiton (1731-1793), botanical superintendent of Kew Gardens for many years, recorded the entrance, the native habitats, and characteristics of the plants, and to these Kew records, he added other information about new introductions obtained while working under Philip Miller at the Chelsea Physick Garden before Kew was founded. In 1789 these records were published in London in three volumes under the title *Hortus Kewensis or a Catalogue of the Plants cultivated in the Royal Botanic Garden at Kew*. In these volumes between five and six thousand plants were arranged according to the Linnaean system, thereby affording a very complete record of the

FLORALIA *A Medley of Blossoms*

blossom arrivals into England during the century.

No colored plates accompanied the text of *Hortus Kewensis*. In the *Botanical Magazine,* however, the prints which appeared from the time it was first published until the death of William Curtis show the beauty of some of the flowers that grew and bloomed in English gardens, though, of necessity, there was a limit to the number of prints included. For his encouragement of exotic botany John Robert Thornton of Clapham deserves particular mention. His garden and hothouses were among the best stocked about London and not only did he grow plants successfully, but he published some illustrated volumes on botany. The most important and pretentious was *The Temple of Flora,* illustrated by twenty-eight beautiful plates. Thornton himself was responsible for one of the illustrations, a group of roses; Sydenham Edwards did another, and the rest were the handiwork of well known artists and engravers of the time.

A more ambitious effort to display the new introductions was made by Henry Andrews when he published in 1797 *The Botanist's Repository for New, and Rare Plants, Containing colored figures of such plants, as have not hitherto appeared in any similar publication; with all their essential characters, botanically arranged, after the sexual system of the celebrated Linnaeus; in English and Latin. To each description is added, a short history of the plant, as to its time of flowering, culture, native place of growth, when introduced, and by whom, the whole executed by Henry Andrews.* Ten volumes make up the

FLORALIA *A Medley of Blossoms*

Botanist's Repository and in each volume there are more than seventy colored plates. From the total of more than seven hundred prints and their accompanying descriptions, one gets an excellent idea of the exotics that the eighteenth century brought to English gardens.

The work of representative plant explorers and collectors has been touched on in earlier chapters and it is of interest to know which of them was responsible for certain introductions. One of the earliest introductions mentioned by Andrews is the rough leaved cordia which Dr. William Sherard brought from Jamaica in 1728. Philip Miller, so well known as a curator of the Chelsea Physick Garden, was one of the first persons in the early part of the century to cultivate the new flowers. Andrews includes a plate of a small climbing blue flower, a native of the East Indies which Miller grew successfully in his greenhouse in 1731. The bird's foot violet, still a favorite among North American wildings, was cultivated in the Physick Garden in 1759 and the cinnamon tree from the Cape of Good Hope was introduced there in 1768.

In Volume I of Andrew's *Repository*, there is a lovely plate of the *Rhododendron punctatum* and the accompanying text says: "It is to the industrious researches of J. Fraser, nurseryman of the King's Road, Chelsea, we are indebted for this charming species of *Rhododendron*, who introduced it in the year 1792 from the back settlements of Carolina, North America, where it is native." Mr. Fraser was credited with numerous other introductions; among them were several whortleberries from Carolina

FLORALIA *A Medley of Blossoms*

about the year 1794, the *Blanfordia cordata,* in 1786, from the banks of the Savannah River in Georgia, and the *Carex,* a curious little plant from Table Mountain near Morgan Town, North Carolina. He brought in the fruitful allspice, a species of *Calycanthus* from Carolina in 1788, which Walter had also recorded in *Flora Caroliniana.* Plate 102 of Volume II is a lovely print of what is commonly known as trailing arbutus, bearing the description: "The Creeping *Epigaea* is the only species of the genus yet in Britain; it was first introduced by P. Collinson, Esq. in 1736, from N. America; where it is found in most parts, from Virginia, as far north as Canada." There is the following note under *"Sarracenia flava* from Carolina in America": "Walter enumerates four species of *Sarracenia* in his *Flora Caroliniana,* all of which exist in London at the present time."

The influence of that noble patron of horticulture, Sir Joseph Banks, was widely felt. From one of his early travels he brought home some lovely varieties of *Arbutus,* and he was also the first to bring the flax from New Zealand. In fact, in all the European gardens were scattered seed brought by his collectors from far distant corners of the earth and these men, too, were largely responsible for the greater part of the many thousands of new plants introduced to English gardens during the reign of George III. No one appears to have more introductions to his credit than Francis Masson, chief collector of Sir Joseph, who, after several years' training at Kew under Aiton, at the age of thirty-one was sent to Africa. He was responsible for several varieties of geraniums, some orchids, the pretty little blue lobelia, arctotis, the calendula, the latter so popular in all gardens now, and many other rare and unusual looking flowers.

Among the most important of the new species, brought from the Cape of Good Hope, were the beautiful *Ericas* which flourished so well under the careful culture received by them in England. This genus became so important that Andrews published *Coloured Engravings of Heaths*. The drawings were taken from living plants only, with specific character, nature, place of growth and time of flowering of each given according to the Linnean system, in Latin and English. This appeared in London over a period from 1802 to 1809. In the preface the author said: "The unabating ardour that still prevails in the science of botany, and rather increases than diminishes, renders it almost impossible for the pencil of the artist to keep pace with the numerous importations from the Cape (at present the sole emporium of the genus *Erica*) . . . The author's intention is, therefore, to figure all the most elegant and desirable of the genus, including many beautiful varieties of recent introduction." The multicolored blossoms, red, yellow, white, lavender, and pink were pleasingly represented in the numerous plates, illustrating the volumes.

From South Africa and the Cape of Good Hope, where Masson and Thunberg, as well as many other astute plant hunters, spent considerable time, numerous contributions were sent to the European gardens between the years 1770 and 1800. Many varieties of gladiolas, the bell flowered

FLORALIA *A Medley of Blossoms*

kind, the cuspidatus, the orchidiflorus, and the ringens or gaping glad, were among those that came from this region during the year mentioned.

The Cape jasmine was a flower whose name was taken from its native habitat (Cape of Good Hope). Linnaeus named this genus (six varieties of which are listed in *Hortus Kewensis*), *Gardenia,* in honor of Dr. Alexander Garden. The first variety introduced to England was *G. aculeata,* in 1733, which was found in the West Indies by Dr. William Houston. From China and Japan in 1754 came the *Gardenia florida* and from the Cape of Good Hope in 1773, the *Gardenia thunbergia.* Francis Masson sent a variety home from the Cape in 1774, and another of Sir Joseph Bank's collectors, John Koenig, sent him one from the East Indies in 1777. A small beautiful flowering variety of gardenia, which "grew naturally" in Carolina was shipped by John Bartram to his friend, Peter Collinson. Linnaeus termed it the *Gardenia fothergilla* to commemorate Dr. Fothergill, although in America it had been called *youngsonia* in honor of William Young, a botanist of Pennsylvania.

The *Geranium,* commonly called wild crane's-bill, although known among the garden flowers of England since the Middle Ages, did not become popular until the latter part of the eighteenth century when many new varieties were brought from South Africa and the Cape of Good Hope. Aiton gives twenty-six varieties with their popular names in *Hortus Kewensis;* among these are the old favorites rather than the new introductions; twelve are listed

FLORALIA *A Medley of Blossoms*

as natives of England and Britain. Mr. John Gerard cultivated the tuberous rooted crane's-bill in 1596; Italy sent one of its natives, streak'd crane's-bill, to England as early as 1629. In her garden in 1704, Her Grace the Duchess of Beaufort grew the hoary crane's-bill, an importation from the Cape of Good Hope; the *Carolina* crane's-bill, the only native from North America, was cultivated in the Chelsea Garden in 1725; and Dr. James Sherard brought the marsh crane's-bill from Germany, its native land, in 1732.

The varieties in *Hortus Kewensis* make an interesting background for the hundreds of new varieties that came from South Africa and the Cape of Good Hope when these sections became favorite hunting grounds for collectors. Andrews must have felt that the new geraniums were too numerous to be dealt with in the *Repository* for he devoted an entire volume to this plant. Just after the end of the century he published in London: *Geraniums or A Monograph of Genus Geraniums Containing Coloured Figures of all Known Species and numerous beautiful varieties Drawn, Engraved, Described and Coloured from the living plants*. In the introduction he says: "It is the author's intention to delineate all the species with their numerous beautiful varieties within the narrowest compass possible by figuring occasionally three or four geraniums on one plate. Introductions from Africa within the last twenty years knew no limits and for which variations we are indebted to the industrious bee; which in its increasing researches after nectariferous juice, constantly conveys pollen, or farrina from one plant to another."

FLORALIA *A Medley of Blossoms*

The popular names given to the "numerous" and "beautiful" varieties are fascinating; they are the marsh crane's-bill, the meadow crane's-bill, the wood crane's-bill, the mountain crane's-bill, the bloody crane's-bill, the hepatica leav'd crane's-bill and the citron-scented crane's-bill. One wonders how so many kinds of crane's-bills could have been given such interesting names. The rose-scented crane's-bill, known now as the rose geranium, was also called the "Otto of Roses" and had been introduced into British gardens in 1690. Another old variety which was cultivated by Miller was the sweet-scented crane's-bill, now called apple geranium. The note under it reads: "It is a desirable plant for any collection. Those who do not admire its scent need not provoke it by rubbing, without which application it is by no means so powerful." There are also many "nose-gay" geraniums which resemble the modern cluster varieties.

Andrews's plates in the Geranium Monograph are lovely to look at. The tones of his colors are much softer than those in the plates of the *Botanist's Repository*. One can understand from the beauty depicted by him why the crane's-bill was one of the popular blossoms of the century and why there is a revival of interest in it today.

Another eighteenth-century introduction which has become more beautiful during all the years until it is one of the most popular flowers at the present time is the dahlia. The first discovered species of this genus known to botanists was the *Dahlia variabilis* which was found in Mexico early in 1789 and named by Cavanilles, a Spanish botanist, in

FLORALIA *A Medley of Blossoms*

honor of another botanist, Dahl, a Swede, who was a pupil of Linnaeus. The old popular name for dahlia was georgina. The plants were sent from a botanic garden in Mexico to the Royal Garden in Madrid, where one of them, *Dahlia pinnata*, flowered in October, 1789. *Dahlia rosea* and *Dahlia coccinea* blossomed a few years later. Seeds from these three plants were sent from Spain to England by Lady Holland to Mr. Buonainti, Lord Holland's librarian in England. From these seeds some excellent plants were produced and the blossoms of *Dahlia pinnata* were a model for Henry Andrews's print in the *Botanist's Repository*.

According to *Hortus Kewensis*, the Marchioness of Bute made the original introduction of the dahlia into England when she brought some plants home from Spain in 1789. Soon after this, Mr. John Fraser obtained some from France, the seed having been sent there from Madrid. The dahlia became a great favorite of the Empress Josephine and its popularity spread over France and into Germany. De Candolle and other students of botany wrote monographs and treatises on the subject, and almost at once many new varieties were produced. It is a far cry, however, from the first little seed which blossomed in Europe to the gorgeous blossoms of today.

There has lately appeared a renewal of interest in many eighteenth-century flowers other than the dahlia and the geranium. The little blue flower which came from Siberia, the *Scilla siberica*, or Siberian squill, is one of the favorites in spring gardens, and the Florida clematis, or large flow-

FLORALIA *A Medley of Blossoms*

ered virgin's-bower, which was sent from Japan to England in 1776, is one variety of a popular genus at the present time.

China was almost as generous as Africa in sharing her plant treasures with Europe. One of her rarest magnolias, *Magnolia fuscata,* found an English home early in the century. Two other interesting and unusual shrubs imported by Sir Abraham Hume were the mandarin orange and the bergamot lemon. China has always been a source of supply of rare and lovely lilies; in 1777, Doctor Fothergill imported one, *Amaryllis fothergillia,* so called in his honor, and in 1791, Sir Joseph Banks was sent by one of his collectors a beautiful, showy lily, which is known today as *Lilium speciosum.*

Perhaps no introduction of the century was more worthy of notice or a more exciting center of interest in the garden world over a long period than the *Camellia japonica.* This flower made one of its early appearances to English botanists in 1702 when James Petiver, apothecary to the Charterhouse, published his *Gasophyllacii Naturae,* a work made up of a series of short descriptions of exotic plants, twenty of which were Chinese. These plants were in a collection made by Dr. James Cunningham, who brought them from China to England, which passed into the possession of Petiver, a friend of many of the distinguished naturalists of that day. From these plants Petiver made his descriptions. He had some Chinese drawings of the plants about which he wrote, and he gave an excellent description of the *Camellia,* although he called it

FLORALIA *A Medley of Blossoms*

The Chinensis Jamaiciensis flore pleno. Kaempfer in 1712 wrote of a visit he made to Japan and mentioned the *Camellia japonica* which he called by the Japanese name of *San-Sa-Tsubaki*. He also records having seen several other varieties of the plant.

It was for Linnaeus to bestow the name *Camellia* when the living plants were brought to England from China in 1739 by a Moravian Jesuit priest, Georges Joseph Kamel. Some traditions hold that Father Kamel died before the turn of the eighteenth century, and that he brought the plant, which became his namesake, to Europe long before that date. Berlese and other students of the *Camellia*, however, accept 1739 as being the date of the introduction of this plant into Europe.

In an early edition of his *Dictionary*, Miller named three species of the *Camellia: Camellia japonica*, or Japan rose; *Camellia sasanqua*, and *Camellia drupifera*. Of it he says: "It is a vast and lofty tree in high esteem with the Japanese for the elegance of its large flower. It is very common everywhere in their groves and gardens, flowering from October to April. It varies with single and double flowers red, white, and purple. It is both wild and cultivated in Cochin-China." In the *Hortus Kewensis*, Aiton names the *Camellia* as a native of China and Japan and says it was cultivated before 1742 by Robert James, Lord Petre.

It is generally accepted that Father Kamel brought home two plants and that they were of the single red variety. Lord Petre bought these plants and, in his endeavor to

FLORALIA *A Medley of Blossoms*

extend hospitality to foreign visitors, gave them too much heat in his greenhouse, with the result that both plants died immediately. His gardener, Gordon, for whom the genus *Gordonia* is named, acquired some camellia plants at a later date, however, which thrived under cooler treatment and set seed. From these, the first English seedlings were raised. In Volume II of a *Natural History of Birds* by George Edwards, there is a colored engraving (Plate 67) of the peacock pheasant from China. The bird is perched on a branch of the camellia on which there are three semi-double pink blossoms. The artist in his descriptive text says: "The flower here figured, by way of decoration is called the Chinese Rose. I drew it from nature; it is what we see most frequently painted in Chinese pictures; it blows broader than a rose, and is of a red rose color, with the stems in the middle of a yellow or gold color. The green leaves are stiff, firm, smooth, like those of evergreens . . . This beautiful flowering tree was raised by the late curious and noble Lord Petre, in his stoves at Thornton-Hall in Essex." At the bottom of the plate appears "Published December 1745 by G. Edwards."

Linnaeus seems to have been responsible for the next importation of camellias. He made great efforts to procure the *Thea* trees for the Botanic Garden at Upsala, and more or less by accident, he brought in the *Camellia japonicas* in the years 1745 and 1769. It is probable that the real cultivation of the camellia in Europe began with the introduction of these plants. It is said that Plate 42 of *Camellia japonica* in Curtis's *Botanical Magazine Vols. 1-2*, pub-

FLORALIA *A Medley of Blossoms*

lished 1787, was made from one of these. This plate, done by William Curtis himself, pictures a single rose-pink flower with anthers standing well out. The paragraph accompanying the plate says: "It is a native of both China and Japan." Thunberg in his *Flora Japonica* (1784) describes it as growing everywhere in the groves and gardens of Japan, where it becomes a prodigiously large and tall tree, highly esteemed by the natives for the elegance of its large and variable blossoms and its evergreen leaves. "Petiver considered this plant as a species of Tea tree— future observations will probably confirm this conjecture." In October, 1763, Linnaeus first received the true tea plant, however, from Gustavus Ekelery, Captain of a Swedish Indiaman, who raised it from seed on the voyage. The first tea plant that flowered in England was at Sion, the seat of the Duke of Northumberland.

A survey of the beauty and variety of flowers that bloomed in English gardens during the latter part of the eighteenth century can be seen in the remarkable portrayals of John Edwards in his *Herbal*. The first edition "containing the most beautiful and scarce flowers and useful medicinal plants which blow in the open air in Great Britain with their Botanical characters; also a Short Account of their Cultivation, etc. etc. The whole corrected according to the latest editions of Botany" was printed for the author in London in 1770.

This volume contains a collection of one hundred colored plates. There are prints of roses, iris, dianthus, anemones, pansies, lupines, single and double daffodils,

FLORALIA *A Medley of Blossoms*

marigolds, sunflowers and hollyhocks. The primulas evidently were as popular then as they are now for Edwards said: "they are so much esteemed in England, and there are so many persons engaged in the culture of this flower." The descriptions which accompany the plates give some interesting notes about the flowers. Under *Convolvulus major,* or heavenly blue morning glory, the text notes this "Annual Bind Weed with Heart shaped leaves or great bindweed ... is an annual plant which grows naturally in Asia and America but has long been cultivated for ornament in English gardens." Many of the flowers pictured herein were natives of the new country across the sea. Following the plate of the *Magnolia grandiflora* is: "This sort grows in Florida and South Carolina."

Because of the excellence of his compositions and the simplicity with which the designs are executed, John Edwards was one of the greatest of English flower print makers. After looking through this beautifully illustrated volume, one has the feeling of having walked through a garden where the flowers had all bloomed in exquisite perfection.

CHAPTER X

"Rose! Thou Art the Sweetest Flower"

"Hail! lovely Rose; of flowers the blushing queen!
Burst, burst, ye nondescripts with spleen!
Ye wondrous nothings, from a foreign soil,
Bought with such labor, care and anxious toil.
Say, can your utmost charms combin'd disclose
Beauty and fragrance equal to the rose?"
    —From the title-page of H. C. Andrews, *Roses*.

SINCE there is a peculiar charm in learning to know something of the customs and ways of life of an epoch long passed away, it is interesting to know some of the myths and symbolical history of the rose, the oldest of celebrated flowers. Sir John Mandeville in his *Travels* tells a story of the origin of roses. A maiden was wrongfully blamed and condemned to be burnt to death on a field called Floridus, which was nigh to Bethlehem. "And as the fire began to burn about her," so the story goes, "she made her prayers to our Lord, that as wisely as she was not guilty of that sin, that he would keep her and make it to be known to all men, of His Merciful Grace. And when she had thus

ONE OF REDOUTÉ'S ROSES

FLORALIA *"Rose! Thou Art the Sweetest Flower"*

said, she entered into the fire, and anon was the fire quenched and out; and the brands that were burning became red Rose trees, and the brands that were not kindled became white Rose trees, full of Roses, And these were the first Rose trees and Roses, both white and red, that every man said; And thus was this maiden saved by the Grace of God. And therefore is that field clept the Field of God Flourished, for it was full of Roses."

There are two references to the rose in the Bible; in the Song of Solomon, Chapter II, Verse 1, is: "I am the rose of Sharon, and the lily of the valleys," and again in Isaiah, Chapter XXXV, Verse 1: "The wilderness and the solitary place shall be glad for them; and the desert shall rejoice and blossom as the rose." It is certain that in Judea the rose bush and its flowers were produced in great perfection. Doubday, an old traveler in the Holy Land, mentions hedges formed of rose bushes, intermingled with pomegranate trees. He states that when the Eastern Christians made one of their processions in the Church of the Holy Sepulchre at Jerusalem, which lasted at least two hours, many men attended it with sacks full of leaves of roses, which they threw by great handfuls on the people. Sandys, another traveler, mentions passing "throw valleys of their Roses voluntarily plentiful." Much use is made of the rose in Christian symbolism.

The rose since the time of Anacreon has been known as the queen of flowers; it was dedicated to Aurora as an emblem of youth, to Venus as an emblem of love and beauty, and to Cupid as one of love and fugacity. Roses were said

FLORALIA *"Rose! Thou Art the Sweetest Flower"*

to be originally white but were changed to red by the blood of Venus when her feet were lacerated by their prickles in her attempt to protect Adonis from the rage of Mars. The rose was a constant companion through life; it was expressive of all that was pleasing to the senses. The early dawn, young life, young love, and a hundred other relations all of a delightful kind are associated with this flower. The Ancients associated it with all their pleasures and sorrows.

Homer speaks of the rose in both the *Iliad* and the *Odyssey*. It was present at every feast, at every time of mirth, and, for the dead, it was twined with the myrtle in token of the future life which was to possess renewed youth and power. The corpse was adorned with it to show a last service of love to the departed. If the body were burned, there were rose leaves and spices mingled with the wine with which the ashes were sprinkled before being placed in the urn.

The Romans understood the art of enjoying to the full every pleasure of life. When mirth had risen high at a feast, they plucked the rose leaves and flung them into the wine, which thus acquired a pleasant taste. At a feast which Cleopatra gave to Antony, she expended immense sums on roses which covered the floor of the banqueting room to the depth of three feet, and over which nets were stretched so as to give elasticity. Roman brides wore wreaths of roses under their purple veils and garlands were showered on the chariots of princes. Graves were adorned with roses, and a beautiful custom consecrated a certain

FLORALIA *"Rose! Thou Art the Sweetest Flower"*
day on which the festival of roses was held for the loved ones who had died.

This flower was extensively employed in the preparation of perfumes, many kinds of foods, and drinks, especially rose wine. Volumes have been written upon its efficacy in medicine, and one of the most earnest defenders of its powers has not hesitated to assure the world that the pharmacopoeia should be formed of roses alone. The chief medicinal use was in the preparation of rose water which was used as a remedy for diseases of the eye. Rose oil and rose water were commonly used as perfumes. Early history claims that roses were among the most potent ingredients of love philters. For the poets the rose has been a mine which all their ingenuity could not exhaust. *"Hommage rendu à la Rose, par le poëtes anciens et modernes, précédé de l'histoire de cette reine des fleurs"*.... Certainly they have always taken account of it in verse and song.

Persuasive spiritual powers were ascribed to the rose. There is a story of a holy virgin named Dorothea who converted a scribe, Theophilus, by sending him some roses in the winter time out of Paradise. The Golden Rose became a symbol of special pontifical favor. Queen Joan of Sicily in 1368 received the Golden Rose from Urban V; and Julius II, as well as Leo X, presented it to Henry VIII of England. In the days of chivalry, roses were worn by cavaliers in tournaments as emblems of their devotion to love and beauty. They have also been the insignia of rival chiefs. The Duke of York in 1452 adopted the white rose, while the Duke of Lancaster had the red rose em-

FLORALIA *"Rose! Thou Art the Sweetest Flower"*
blazoned on his shield. The rose striped with red and white is to this day called the York and Lancaster rose.

The oldest monograph on the rose is by Nicol Monardes, a physician who died at Seville about 1577, which was published by the celebrated Clusius, at Antwerp in 1565 under the title, *De Rosa et partibus ejus*. The rose books of the eighteenth century were, however, a rather new and more elaborate conception than the earlier publications on this genus.

In speaking of these books Dr. John Sims in the *Annals of Botany*, Vol. I, said: "Though prose as well as poetry may have from time immemorial joined in proclaiming the Rose the queen of flowers, yet so little homage has been paid to her by botanists that, generally speaking, she may still be pronounced the very opprobrium of the sciences." Although the writer welcomed the new interest manifested in this flower, he was highly critical of some of the publications that appeared. He went on to say: "The latest publications on this genus are Guillemau's *Natural History of the Rose* and Rossig's *Description of Roses*. Both bear evident marks of superficial observation, are mere compilations, void of criticism and, therefore, of little use to those who wish to become scientifically acquainted with the species they cultivate. The former of these authors has moreover revived even the fabulous accounts of imaginary species; yet his work may be said to be a somewhat more amusing compilation than that of Mr. Rossig. *Roses Drawn and Coloured After Nature*, by the latter, of which there are five numbers, each containing five plates, with

FLORALIA *"Rose! Thou Art the Sweetest Flower"*

short descriptions in German and French, is a publication not devoid of merit. The strictures, however, which the preface contains on Miss Lawrance's *Collection of Roses* are uncandid; for, to speak the truth, in point of botanical merit, this lady's performance is nearly on a par with Mr. Rossig's own work, and its execution is superior."

The spirit of criticism and jealousy which Mr. Rossig shows concerning Miss Lawrance's work seems, unfortunately, to have been a characteristic of the artists of the period. The development of magnanimity of soul and generosity of appreciation toward one's fellow artists evidently did not keep pace with the development of artistic aptitudes, for in each of the books with which this article deals there is evidence that the author bears malice to others working in the same field. As a matter of fact, Mary Lawrance's *Collection of Roses from Nature* has been recognized through the years as one of the rare volumes on this subject, and certainly it is a superior work to that of Mr. Rossig. He published *Die Rosen* in two volumes in 1812 and 1820 and so had the advantage of commenting on *Roses from Nature*, which was published in London just before the end of the century. From 1796 to 1799, Miss Lawrance published a series of plates illustrating the various kinds of roses cultivated in England, drawn from nature. Critics feel that while they are not botanically accurate they are remarkably beautiful. There are some lists at the end of the volume, but other than these no text accompanies the plates. Fairy roses or *Rosa laurenciana*, sixteen varieties of dwarf plants which are perfectly

FLORALIA *"Rose! Thou Art the Sweetest Flower"*

symmetrical in form with diminutive rosebuds of exquisite color, named for Miss Lawrance by her friend Robert Sweet, perpetuate her name today.

In point of time the next rose book to appear was in 1805 when Henry C. Andrews published Volume I of his *Roses: or A Monograph of the Genus Rosa, containing colored figures of all the known species and beautiful varieties drawn, engraved, described and colored from the Living Plants.* In the introduction of this volume the author gives as his purpose in bringing it forth: "The arrangement as accurately as possible of the numerous beautiful varieties, with their species—an arduous task considering the neglect they have experienced and the wild and indiscriminate manner in which they have been profusely mixed. The extent of the genus has been most vaguely estimated; by some enumerated at two hundred and forty ... But we think a rational computation would confine them within a hundred, including every distinct variety ... As the merits of the present undertaking may easily be appreciated by a free access to all its beautiful originals, the author hopes a candid allowance will be made, upon a comparison with the living plant, when it is considered that the most elaborate efforts of art have never yet been able to do justice to its superior beauty."

The second volume of *Monograph of the Genus Rosa* was published some years later. The author states in the preface to this volume that the factitious increase of the genus *Rosa* during the twenty years that had elapsed since the publication of the first volume had increased twofold.

FLORALIA *"Rose! Thou Art the Sweetest Flower"*

In speaking of the contents of the two volumes he says: "We have separated the work into Two Parts or Volumes: the First containing all the larger Roses, such as *Provincialis, centifolia,* and *Damask* species or monthly roses natives of Britain and the South of Europe. The second Volume includes nearly all of the smaller Roses, as the *Eglanterias* or Sweet-briars, *Spinossimas* or Scotch roses: also those denominated China or Indian Roses, so distinct from the European species." There is a colored plate for every rose which he mentions and on the page opposite the plate is the name of the species and also "specific character" in Latin and in English. Then follows a short descriptive paragraph giving the author's personal evaluation of the variety. He also gives the place from which the particular rose was imported or originated, where it first flowered and interesting bits of history about it.

Because the drawings were carefully made and the coloring rather gorgeous and deep, many of the Andrews plates are very decorative. However, they are line engravings and on some of the plates the lines are so heavy that they almost spoil the beauty of the flowers. Many of the illustrations were done on double sheets; and some of these sheets show two or three varieties of roses. The plates of *Rosa muscosa,* or moss rose, are particularly interesting. These are the single moss rose, moss provence rose, the pale flower moss provence rose, the white or bath moss rose, and many others. The moss provence was supposed by Linnaeus to be the only variety of the *Rosa centifolia.* In striking contrast to the moss roses, Andrews gives a

FLORALIA *"Rose! Thou Art the Sweetest Flower"*

plate of *Rosa inermis,* or rose without thorns, and he says of it: "This thornless rose may be almost considered as the exception to the otherwise general rule; a specific so unequivocally good seldom occurs." The eglantines, or *Rosa eglanteria,* formed a large group, and for these Mr. Andrews evidently had much affection for he quite bursts into enthusiastic praise when he describes them. "It is an old inhabitant of the gardens and will always continue to be one of its sweetest ornaments." He quotes the poet who says:

"How sweet is the Eglantine breeze!
The very name sounds dulcet to our ear!"

However, this artist came in for his share of criticism from his contemporaries. Sims damned him with mild praise when he spoke of one of his contributions as "a work where the author struggles, with considerable success, to compensate for the total absence of science." Whereupon Andrews retaliated with a long and violent attack. He concluded one statement with: "It is much better to try one's own strength, however weak, than to remain tottering between the support of two unequal crutches."

But it was for Dr. John Lindley, a well known botanist and garden author who was for a long time associated with the Royal Society, to set all the would-be authorities straight in his *Rosarum Monographia: or A Botanical History of Roses.* In the preface he apologizes for bringing forth another book when "the number of publications on this present subject is already too considerable," but, he

FLORALIA *"Rose! Thou Art the Sweetest Flower"*

says, "nothing is more notorious than the almost inextricable confusion in which Roses are to this day involved." One feels that Dr. Lindley's monograph was brought out as a rebuke to those who had previously published rose books. He evidently felt that he had done a very good job for he concludes his preface by saying: "If I have in some measure succeeded I shall have the satisfaction of knowing that the way for whome so ever may succeed me will be less impassable."

Dr. Lindley claimed that half of the species had been found in Asia and that it might be called "The Land of the Rose." Europe had at the time of his writing twenty-five species, China fifteen, and perhaps many more undescribed species, and Persia six. The Chinese and Indian are entirely different from the rest. North Africa had two species peculiar to that country and two others common to it and Europe. Fourteen species have been found in North America, none of which except *Rosa montezumae* and *Rosa stricta,* have much general resemblance to European roses. "It is not," he says, "unworthy of notice that *R. laevigate* of the woods of Georgia is so similar to the *R. sinica* of China as not to be immediately distinguishable from it. The latter is even sold in some of the London nurseries as an American Rose under the name R. Cherokeensis." He goes on to tell further that "It is a mistake to suppose that double roses are of somewhat modern origin; since they are particularly mentioned by Herodotus, and Pliny enumerates several sorts, among which is the *centifolia.*"

Dr. Lindley was so well known for his writing over a

FLORALIA *"Rose! Thou Art the Sweetest Flower"*

wide range of botanical subjects that his ability as an artist was apt to be overlooked. His volume on the rose contains nineteen plates, most of which he did himself. In 1859 the Royal Horticultural Society, because of a financial crisis, had to liquidate its assets, most important of which were the library and the collection of prints. Among the most valuable series of the latter that were sold were Dr. Lindley's original drawings for his *Rosarum Monographia.* This loss was considered irreplaceable as these prints were among the society's treasured possessions. However, by chance, in recent years these drawings came on the market and were purchased and again put in the library of the society.

The last of the rose books to appear was that of the French painter of flowers, Pierre Joseph Redouté. *Les Roses,* which was described in an earlier chapter, makes one feel that the purpose of all flower painting before his time was to show by comparison the beauty and wonder of his work. The perfection of his designs, the transparent tone which gave a lifelike quality to the foliage, and the exquisite coloring of the blossoms, which came from his own method of engraving (unfortunately lost to us) entitle the creator of this beauty to wear the crown as *artiste supérieur de la rose.*

Dr. Lindley, for all his assurance in having set the world right about roses, is held up for some inadequacies in his *Rosarum Monographia.* Mr. Thory in his description of *Rosa hudsoniana* has this to say: "Mr. J. Lindley in his *monographie de genre rosier* which he published in

FLORALIA *"Rose! Thou Art the Sweetest Flower"*

October, 1820 . . . spoke of *R. carolina* as the same thing as our rose d'Hudson. It is evident that he has never seen the latter living or dead. We invite him to read the description which we have given of the *R. hudsoniana* and to study the figure which accompanies it."

The Redouté rose volumes were brought out in three editions, and from the time of their publication down to the present, the claim has been conceded that they are the most beautiful books about the most beautiful flower. Both the artist and the author displayed their talents in a most remarkable manner, and one believes that the names of Redouté and Thory will be among the immortals.

Because it is a flower of beauty and grace, the rose has contributed to the enjoyment of life from the time of the Ancients. Octave Delepierre in an essay on the history of the rose expressed a meaning that it might have for the future: "We have seen that the rose is the symbol of youth and the freshness of life. If we are honestly anxious, each in his sphere, to advance horticulture in our land, and thus contribute to beautifying the world of flowers, and to increasing the delight in the Nature that lies around us, the Rose may henceforth be to our society the symbol of the ever fresh vigour with which we press towards the fair goal which is set before us."

BIBLIOGRAPHY

BIBLIOGRAPHY

CHAPTER I

Abercrombie, John. *Every Man his Own Gardener.* London, 1794.

Bradley, Richard. *The Gentleman and Gardener's Kalendar.* London, 1718.

———, *New Improvements of Planting and Gardening both Philosophical and Practical.* 7th ed., London, 1739.

———, *A General Treatise of Agriculture.* 1723.

British Museum. *Memorials of Linnaeus.* London, 1907.

Forsyth, William. *A Treatise on the Culture and Management of Fruit Trees.* American ed., Albany, 1803.

Jackson, B. D. *Guide to the Literature of Botany.* London, 1881.

Johnson, George W. *A History of English Gardening.* London, 1829.

Lawrence, John. *The Fruit Garden Kalendar.* London, 1718.

———, *The Lady's Recreation in the Art of Gardening.* London, 1717.

Linnaean Society of London. *Charter and By-Laws.* London, 1861.

Rockley, A.M. Cecil. *A History of Gardening in England.* 2nd ed., London, 1896; 3rd ed., London, 1910.

FLORALIA *Bibliography*

Society of Gardeners. *Catalogus Plantarum*. London, 1730.

Stoever, D. H. *The Life of Sir Charles Linnaeus*. London, 1794.

Switzer, Stephen. *Ichnographia Rustica*. London, 1718.

CHAPTER II

Addison, Joseph. "An Essay on the Pleasures of the Garden," *Spectator*, No. 477.

———, "Description of a Garden in the Natural Style," *Spectator*, No. 414.

Chambers, Sir William. *A Dissertation on Oriental Gardening*. London, 1772.

Gilpin, William. *Three Essays*. London, 1792.

Gothein, Marie Louise. *A History of Garden Art*. New York, 1928.

Hazlitt, W. Carew. *Gleanings in Old Garden Literature*. London, 1887.

Johnson, George W. *A History of English Gardening*. London, 1829.

Langley, Batty. *New Principles of Gardening*. London, 1728.

Nichols, Rose Standish. *English Pleasure Gardens*. New York, 1902.

Pope, Alexander. "Essay on Verdant Sculpture," *The Guardian*, No. 173.

Price, Sir Uvedale. *An Essay on the Picturesque*. London, 1794-98.

Repton, Humphrey. *Observations on the Theory and Practice of Landscape Gardening*. London, 1797.

FLORALIA *Bibliography*

Rockley, A.M. Cecil. *A History of Gardening in England.* London, 1896, 1910.

Shenstone, William. "Unconnected Thoughts on Gardening," *Works in Verse and Prose of William Shenstone.* 2nd ed., London, 1765.

Sieveking, Albert Forbes. *The Praise of Gardens—An Epitome of the Literature of Garden Art.* London, 1899.

Switzer, Stephen. *The Nobleman, Gentleman and Gardener's Recreation.* London, 1715.

Walpole, Horace, "Essay on Modern Gardening," *The Works of Horace Walpole.* London, 1785.

CHAPTER III

Fairchild, Thomas. *The City Gardener.* London, 1722.

Furber, Robert. *The Flower Garden Display'd.* London, 1732-34.

———, "Catalogue," *The Gardener's and Florist's Dictionary,* by Philip Miller, Vol. II, appendix. London, 1724.

Johnson, George W. *A History of English Gardening.* London, 1829.

Journal of Horticulture, LVI (1876. Old Series, XXXI), 76-78.

Miller, Philip. "An Account of Some Experiments Relating to the Flowering of Tulips, Narcissus, etc. in Winter by Placing Their Bulbs upon Glasses of Water," *Philosophical Transactions of the Royal Society,* XXXVII, 81-84. London, 1733.

———, *Figures of the Most Beautiful, Useful and Uncom-*

mon Plants Described in the Gardener's Dictionary. London, 1760.

———, Gardener's Dictionary. London, 1731-1807. There were many editions as follows: 1st ed., 1731—reissue Dublin, 1732; 2nd ed., corrected, 1733—appendix, 1735, 22 pp; 3rd ed., corrected, 1737; 2nd vol., 1739; 2nd vol., 2nd ed., 1740; 4th ed. (two), Dublin, 1741 —London, 1741; 4th ed., corrected, 1743; 5th ed., 1748; 6th ed., 1752 (1st complete ed.); 7th ed., 1759; 8th ed., 1768; German ed., 1750-58; French ed., 1785; another ed., ed. Thomas Martyn, London, 1807.

———, The Gardener's Kalendar. London, 1732, 1737, 1743.

———, The Method of Cultivating Madder. London, 1758.

———, "Method of Raising Some Exotick Seeds," Philosophical Transactions of the Royal Society, XXXV, 485-88. London, 1729.

———, (trans.) Elements of Agriculture, by H. L. Duhamel du Monceau. London, 1764.

Rockley, A.M. Cecil. *A History of Gardening in England.* London, 1896, 1910.

Rogers, John. *The Vegetable Cultivator.* London, 1843.

Sargent, Charles Sprague. *The Silva of North America*, I, 38. Boston, 1891-1902.

Society of Gardeners. *Catalogus Plantarum.* London, 1730.

CHAPTER IV

Banks, Sir Joseph. *Illustrations of Australian plants collected in 1770.* London, 1900-1905.

FLORALIA *Bibliography*

———, *A Short Account of the Diseases of Corn.* London, 1805.
Banks, Sir Joseph, and the Royal Society. London, 1844.
Blunt, Reginald. *By Chelsea Reach.* London, 1921.
Johnson, George W. *A History of English Gardening.* London, 1829.
Rockley, A.M. Cecil. *A History of Gardening in England.* London, 1896.
Sloane, Sir Hans. *Catalogus Plantarum quae in insula Jamaica sponte proveniunt.* London, 1696.
Smith, Edward. *Life of Sir Joseph Banks.* London, 1911.
Society of Gardeners. *Catalogus Plantarum.* London, 1730.

CHAPTER V

Bartram, William. *Travels through North and South Carolina.* Philadelphia, 1791.
Burnaby, Rev. Andrew. *Travels through the Middle Settlements in North America in the Years 1759 and 1760.* London, 1775.
Catesby, Mark. *The Natural History of Carolina.* London, 1731-43.
Chastellux, Le Marquis de. *Voyages ... dans l'Amerique Septentrionale dans les années 1780, 1781, 1782,* Vols. I-II. Paris, 1786.
Clayton, John. *Flora Virginica—Exhibens Plantas.* Leyden, 1739.
Coker, W. C. *A Visit to the Grave of Thomas Walter.* Raleigh, N. C., 1910.

FLORALIA *Bibliography*

Crèvecoeur, Saint John de. *Letters from an American Farmer*. Dublin and London, 1782.

Cutler, Manasseh. *Plants of New England*. Cincinnati, 1903. Reprint of 1785 publication.

Darlington, William. *Memorials of John Bartram and Humphry Marshall*. Philadelphia, 1849.

Garden, Alexander. *An Account of the Pink Root with its Uses as a Vermifuge*. 1764.

Gee, Wilson P. *South Carolina Botanists*. New York, 1918.

Jefferson, Thomas. *Notes on the State of Virginia*. Richmond, 1852. A new edition: notes first written 1781 —enlarged 1782.

John Bartram Association. *Bartram's Garden*. Philadelphia, 1904 and 1907.

Kalm, Peter. *Travels into North America*. Trans. by J. R. Forster Warrington. London, 1770-71.

Lawson, John. *A New Voyage to Carolina*. London, 1709.

Logan, Martha. *A Gardener's Calendar*. [early 1750's].

Maxon, William R. "Thomas Walter, Botanist," *Smithsonian Miscellaneous Collections*, Vol. XCV, No. 8. Washington, 1937.

Michaux, André. "Journal," *Proceedings of the American Philosophical Society* [Boston, 1888].

Randolph, John. *A Treatise on Gardening*. Georgetown, D. C., 1818. Original date unknown.

Squibb, Robert. *The Gardener's Kalendar for South Carolina, Georgia and North Carolina*. Charleston, 1787.

Torrey, John. *Catalogue of Natural History of New York*. New York, 1819.

Walter, Thomas. *Flora Caroliniana*. London, 1788.

CHAPTER VI

Boutcher, William. *A Treatise on Forest-Trees*. Edinburgh, 1775.

Catesby, Mark. *Hortus Britanno-Americanus*. London, 1737.

Darlington, William. *Memorials of John Bartram and Humphry Marshall*. Philadelphia, 1849.

Duhamel du Monceau, Henri Louis. *La Physique des Arbres*. Paris, 1758.

Gilpin, William. *Remarks on Forest Scenery*. London, 1791.

Gray, Christopher. *A Catalogue of Trees and Shrubs (Magnolia Altissima)*. London, 1740.

Kennion, Edward. *An Essay on Trees in Landscape*. London, 1815.

Knoop, Johann Herman. *Dendrologia*. Leeuwarden, 1763.

Marshall, Humphry. *Arbustrum Americanum*. Philadelphia, 1785.

Michaux, André, *L'Histoire des Chênes de l'Amérique*. Paris, 1801.

Wade, Walter. *Quercus; or, Oaks*. Dublin, 1809.

Wangenheim, Friedrich Adam Julius von. *Beschreibung einiger nordamerikanischen Holz- und Buscharten*. Göttingen, 1781.

Weston, Richard. *The Gardener's and Planter's Calendar*. London, 1778.

FLORALIA *Bibliography*

CHAPTER VII

Curtis, William. *The Botanical Magazine.* Vols. I-XIV (1787-1800). London.

———, *Directions for Cultivating the Crambe Maritima.* London, 1822.

———, *Flora Londinensis.* London, 1777.

———, *Lectures on Botany.* London, 1803-04.

———, *Practical Observations on the British Grasses* (4th ed.). London, 1805.

Nelmes, Ernest (comp.). *Portraits and Biographical Notes, Curtis's Botanical Magazine Dedications.* London, 1931.

CHAPTER VIII

Bouchard-Huzard, Louis. "Notice Nécrologique sur M. Redouté," *Annales Société Royal D'Horticulture de Paris,* Vol. XXVII (1840).

Duhamel du Monceau, Henri Louis. *Traité des Arbres et Arbustes que l'on cultive en France en pleine terre.* Paris, [1800]-1819.

Redouté, Pierre Joseph. *Album de Redouté, peintre de fleurs.* [Paris, 18—].

———, *Choix des plus belles roses, peintes d'apres Nature, imprimées en couleur et retouchees au pinceau.* Paris, 1845.

———, *Les Liliacées.* Paris, 1802-16.

———, *Les Roses, peintes par P. J. Redouté.* Paris, 1824.

Rousseau, Jean Jacques, *La Botanique.* Paris, 1805.

FLORALIA *Bibliography*

Seringe, N. C. *Musée Helvétique d'histoire naturelle.* Berne, 1823.

Woodward, B. B. "Redouté's Works," *Journal of Botany— British and Foreign,* Vol. XLIII (1905).

CHAPTER IX

Aiton, William. *Hortus Kewensis.* London, 1789.

Andrews, Henry. *The Botanist's Repository.* London, 1797.

———, *Coloured Engravings of Heaths.* London, 1802-09.

———, *Geraniums.* London, 1805.

Curtis, William, *The Botanical Magazine,* Vols. I-XIV (1787-1800). London.

Edwards, John. *Herbal.* London, 1770.

Hanbury, William. *A Complete Body of Planting and Gardening.* London, 1771.

Johnson, George W. *The Dahlia.* London, 1847.

Thunberg, Karl Peter. *De Gardenia.* Upsala, 1780.

CHAPTER X

Andrews, Henry C. *Roses: or Monograph of the Genus Rosa.* London, 1805.

Delepierre, Joseph Octave. *An Essay on the Mythological and Symbolical History of the Rose.* London, [1856].

Lindley, Joseph. *Rosarum Monographia: or, A Botanical History of Roses.* London, 1820.

Redouté, Pierre Joseph. *Les Roses, peintes par P. J. Redouté.* Paris, 1824.

Shaw, Henry. *The Rose, Historical and Descriptive: gathered from various sources.* St. Louis, 1879.

Wellcome, Mrs. M. *An Essay on Roses Historically and Descriptively Considered.* Yarmouth, Me., [1881].

INDEX

INDEX

Abercrombie, John, *Every Man His Own Gardener, etc.*, 12
Acacia, 39-40, 81, 102
Academy of Sciences of Sweden, 4
Adam, Pilinski, bookmaker, 135
Addison, pioneer of Naturalistic School, 20, 21; country place at Bilton, 23; on gardening, 25
Agricultural Society of Charleston, 92
Aiton, William, 66, 109, 141; *Hortus Kewensis*, 16, 138-39, 143, 144, 146, 148; Kew records of, 138
Alaternus (evergreen), 46
Alchorne, Mr., on Curtis, 114
Almond tree, 105
Alston, John, 35
Al-z, Iw-n, 71, 72, 73
American Philosophical Society, 93
André, painter, 128
Andrews, Henry C., *Botanist's Repository*, 139-40, 144, 145; *Coloured Engravings of Heaths*, 142; *Geraniums*, 144; *Roses, etc.*, 152, 158-59, 160
Anemones, 150
Anne, Queen, 31, 60
Antwerp, 156
Apothecaries' Hall, in London, 54
Arbustrum Americanum. See Marshall
Arbutus, 46, 141
Arctotis, 142
Ardennes, 127
Argyle, Duke of, 53
Ash, 98, 99
Ashley River, 92, 102
Asparagus, 11, 12
Atamasco lily, 75, 81
Atkyns, *Gloucester, etc.*, 32
Audubon, John James, 127, 129, 137
Augusta, Dowager Princess of Wales, 15

Bacon, Stephen, 36
Badminton, Duchess of Beaufort's gardens at, 53

Banana tree, 99
Banks, Lady, 135
Banks, Sir Joseph, 16, 135, 141, 143, 147; ancestry, boyhood, and education, 62; scientific expedition to Newfoundland, 63; farming activities, 64; friendship with Lord Sandwich, 64; trip on "Endeavour," 64-65; herbarium, 65; honors, death, 66; various interests, 67; instructions to new collectors, 67-68; encouragement of Curtis's work, 115
Banks, Sir William, 63
Bartolozzi, Italian engraver, 126
Bartram, John, 79, 87, 93, 103, 104, 109, 143; builds first greenhouse in America, 10; correspondence with Collinson, 14; Al-z on, 71-72, 73; first interest in botany, 73-75; influence of Collinson on, 75; correspondents, 76; observation on pollen grains, 77; death, 77; friendship with Peter Kalm, 78; collecting for friends, 83
Bartram, William, "Billy," 77, 93, 104; travels and diary, 89-90; publications, 90
Bauhin, Gaspar, *Pinax*, 55
Bay (evergreen), 46
Beans, 11
Beaufort, Duchess of, 144; as collector of rare plants, 53
Belgians, Queen of the, 135
"Bell-glasses," 11
Belvoir Castle, of Duke of Rutland, 9
Berkenhout, botanical lexicon of, 111
Berlese, student of Camellias, 148
Bermondsey, Curtis's garden at, 114, 121
Berry, Duchess de, 132, 135
Bertram. *See* Bartram
Bickerstaff, Thomas, 36
Bilton, Addison's country place at, 23
Blanfordia cordata, 141
Blenheim, estate at, 29, 33

179

FLORALIA *Index*

Bligh, Captain William, 67, 68-69
Bolabola, 68
Boldre, Gilpin at, 33
Bonafous, friend of Redouté, 133, 137
Bonplaud, A., Redouté illustrated book of, 133
Botanical Magazine. See Curtis, William
Botanic Garden, of Chelsea, 15, 45, 46, 54, 144; at Kew, 15, 16; at Cambridge, 16; at Kensington, 41; at Calcutta, 67; on Schuylkill River, 76; at Marshallton, 103; at Upsala, 149
Botanist's Repository. See Andrews
"Bounty," 67, 68
Box (evergreen), 46
Boyle, Robert, 54
Bradley, Richard, writings, 7-8; death, 8, 10; *Works of Nature*, 9; forcing of plants, 9; admirer of Fairchild, 40, 41
Breadfruit tree, 65, 67, 68, 69
Bridgeman, 22; and natural gardens, 20; Ha-Ha style, 25-26
British grasses, 116-17, 118
British Museum, founded by Sloane, 54, 64; beginnings of, 60, 61
Brompton, Curtis's garden at, 116
Brown, Lancelot, "Capability Brown," garden designer, 31; criticism of, 31-32
Bulbs, flower, in water, 49
Bull, Colonel, plantation of, 102
Buonainti, Mr., Lord Holland's librarian, 146
Burleigh, estate mentioned by Gilpin, 33
Burnaby, Rev. Andrew, early traveler in America, 80-81
Bute, Lord, 15
Bute, Marchioness of, 146
Byrd, Colonel W., 76

Calcutta Botanic Garden, 67
Calendars, fruit-garden, 9; for gardeners, 10, 12, 42-45, 49, 95
Calendula, 142
Calycanthus, 141
Cambridge, 8, 62; botanical garden at, 16
Camellias, 147-48, 149
Candolle, A. P., writes text of Les Liliacées of Redouté, 133; on *Dahlias*, 146
Cape Jasmine. *See* Gardenia

Cape of Good Hope, 140, 142, 143; collecting trips to, 65, 66
Carex, 141
Carnation, 96
Castlehill, estate mentioned by Gilpin, 33
Catalogue, of flowers, 36, 43-45, 95; of plants, 36, 42, 56, 95, 138; of trees, 36, 42, 46, 94, 104, 106; of Lambeth Marsh garden, 115-16
Catalogus Plantarum. See Sloane, and Society of Gardeners
Catesby, Mark, 93; sent seeds from Carolina, 40; dedicated book to Sloane, 59; voyage to Virginia, 83; second trip to Virginia, 84-86; trip to Bahama Islands, 86; *Natural History of Carolina, etc.*, 86, 87-88; death, 88; *Hortus Britanno-Americanus*, 88, 100-2
Cauliflower, 11, 96
Cavanilles, Spanish botanist, 145
Cedars, 80, 83
Cedrus Montis Libani, 46
Celsius, Olaf, Swedish botanist, 4
Cemetery du Pere-La-Chaise, 137
Centifolia. See Roses
Chambers, Sir William, 32; advocate of Chinese methods, 29-30; on landscape gardening, 31
Chamoedaphnes, 81
Chaptal, French statesman, 133
Château de Calsbourg, Redouté works in, 128
Chelsea Physick Garden, 59, 138, 140, 144
Chemists, contribution to horticulture, 7
Chestnuts, scarlet-flowering, 81
Chinese gardens, 30, 32
Cinnamon tree, 140
City Gardener. See Fairchild
Claremont, estate mentioned by Whateley, 29
Classicism, in garden design, 19-20
Clayton, Dr. John, Collinson on, 79; Jefferson's tribute to, 80
Clematis, 146
Clusius, publisher of Monardes' *De Rosa et partibus ejus*, 156
Cocoanut palm, 65
Cocoa tree, 99
Colden, Dr. Cadwallader, early work on botany, 79
Coldenham, Dr. Colden's home at, 79
Cole, Richard, 36

FLORALIA *Index*

Collecting expeditions, 65, 66, 67, 92, 141
College of Physicians, 56, 59, 60, 84
Collinson, Peter, 10, 79, 141, 143; introduces new plants, 14; friendship with Bartram, 14; and Benjamin Franklin, 14; influence on Bartram, 75
Collinsonia Canadensis, 14
Colliton, Sir John, Bart., 102
Colonists, early, 16
Color printing, 126
Compton, Dr., 53
Cook, Captain James, 64, 65
Copper plates, 47, 90, 126
Cordia, rough-leaved, 140
Cornwallis, Lord, 67
Court of the Apothecaries Company, 59
Courten, William, collection of, 57
Crabtree, Philippa, artist, 125
Crambe maritima (sea kale), 116, 118
Crane's-bill. *See* Geranium
Crèvecoeur, Saint John de, 71, 75
Cucumbers, 11, 45, 96
Cumberland, Duke of, 53
Cunningham, Dr. James, 147
Curtis, Samuel, 125
Curtis, William, boyhood, 111; friendship with Legg, 111; schooling, 111-12; botanical assistant, 112-13, 119; practiced medicine, 113; devoted himself to botany, 113-14; interest in medicinal plants, 114-15; plants at Lambeth Marsh, 115-16; moved to Brompton, 116; book on British grasses, 116-17; publishing activities, 116, 117, 118, 119; on sea kale, 118-19; memoirs, 119; *Lectures on Botany,* 110, 125; delivers lectures, 119, 124; *Flora Londinensis,* and other publications, 120, 121-25; break with Linnean Society, 123; *Botanical Magazine,* 123-24, 125, 149-50; death, 124, 125, 139
Custis, Colonel, John Bartram corresponds with, 76
Cutler, Rev. Manasseh, New England botanist, 79
Cypress, 80

Daffodils, 150
Dahl, Swedish botanist, 146
Dahlia, 145, 146
Dahoon holly, 102

Darlington, William, 80
Date trees, 99
Delepierre, Octave, essayist, 163
Desfontaines, Redouté illustrates work of, 132
Devonshire, Colliton's garden at, 102
Dianthus, 150
Didot, publisher of Redouté's *Les Roses,* 134
Dillenius, John James, 52, 76, 111
Dissections, botanical, 48
Dogwood, 81, 87
Doubday, traveler in Holy Land, 153
Driver, Samuel, 36
Duforty, Monsieur, lecturer at Hospital of La Charité, 55
Du Fresnoy, director of garden at Versailles, 20
Duhamel du Monceau, Henri Louis, 109, 133; *La Physique des Arbres: etc.,* 107
Duilhier, Nicholas Facio, 9; *Fruit Walls, etc.,* 9-10

East India Company, 67
East Indies, 140, 143
Eaton, Joseph Banks in school at, 62
Edwards, George, 87, 88, 149; on Sloane, 59-60
Edwards, John, *Herbal,* 150-51
Edwards, Sydenham Taste, artist, 122, 124, 139
Ekelery, Captain Gustavus, 150
Elémens de botanique. See Tournefort
Ellis, William, 12, 13
Elm, 96, 98, 99
Else, Mr., 112
Eltham. *See* Sherard, James
"Endeavour," 64, 65
Enfield, home of Dr. Uvedale at, 53
Epigaea. See Arbutus
Ericas, 142
Evelyn, John, 58; influence on Bradley, 7; influence on Miller, 49; and Courten collection, 57
Evergreens, 46
Exmouth, Colliton's garden at, 102
"Exoticks," 15, 38, 41, 42, 49, 52, 53, 58, 101, 103, 138, 140, 147

Fairchild, Thomas, 35; experiments. 40; *City Gardener,* 41; death and will, 41; "Fairchild Lectures," 41
Farmer King. *See* George III

181

FLORALIA *Index*

Favens, Monsieur, professor at Hospital of La Charité, 55
Fig tree, 105
Flalia (evergreen), 46
Flanders, Redouté in, 128
Flax plants, 68, 141
Flora Caroliniana. See Walter
Flora Japonica. See Thunberg
Flora Lapponica. See Linnaeus
Flora Londinensis. See Curtis, William
Flower Garden Display'd. See Furber
Fordyce, Dr., lecturer on Anatomy, 112
Fothergill, Dr., 143, 147; on Collinson, 14; as early gardener, 53; as patron of William Bartram, 89
Franklin, Benjamin, 14, 89
Franklinia alatamaha, 89, 104
Fraser, John, 91, 140-41, 146
French Academy of Sciences, 60
French missionaries, 82
Fringe-trees, 81
Fruit Garden Kalendar. See Lawrence
Fruit wall, 9-10
Fulham, Bishop of London's garden at, 39, 53
Furber, Robert, 35, 40, 87; founder of nursery at Kensington, 41; *Catalogue of Curious Trees and Plants*, 42-44; *Flower Garden Display'd*, 43-44, 49; on growing bulbs on water, 49

Garden, Dr. Alexander, 76; education and travels of, 88; publications and honors, 88-89; *Gardenia* named for, 89, 143
Gardener's and Florist's Dictionary. See Miller, Philip
Gardener's Chronicle, article on Philippa Crabtree in, 124
Gardener's Dictionary. See Miller, Philip
Gardener's Kalendar. See Miller, Philip
Gardenia, 89, 143
Gardening, books on, 12; landscape, 35
Gardens, affected by times, 17-18; kitchen, 10-11, 35; vegetable, 11, 12
Genera Plantarum. See Linnaeus
George III, the Farmer King, 15, 16, 64, 141

Geranium, 142, 143-45
Gerard, John, 111; *Herbal*, 62; cultivated crane's-bill, 144
Gilpin, William, influence on national taste, 33-34, 96-97; *Remarks on Forest Scenery, etc.*, 97-98
Gladiolas, 142
Golden Rose, 155
Goodricke, Sir Henry, letter to Sloane, 58-59
Gordon, gardener to Lord Petre, 149
Gordonia and *Gordonia lasianthus*, 89
Grange Road Garden, Curtis's first botanic garden, 114, 115
Gray, Christopher, 29, 36, 101; on *Magnolia altissima*, 94-95
Greenhouse, 11, 42, 47, 68, 95, 103, 123, 140, 149; evolution of, 9-10
Green Privet (evergreen), 46
Gronovius, Professor J. F., correspondent of Bartram, 76; classified Virginia plants, 79-80; named plant for Catesby, 88; botanical system of, 106, 108
Guardian, The, 21
Guillemau, *Natural History of the Rose*, 156

Ha-Ha style, of Bridgeman, 25; used by Washington, 26
Hanover, Elector of, 13
Harderwyk, University of, 5
Harrow, Joseph Banks a student at, 62
"Haw-Ha!" See Ha-Ha
Hemlock, 114
Henry VIII, 155
Herbal. See Edwards, John, and Gerard, John
Herodotus, 161
Hill, Dr. John. See Hill, Sir John
Hill, Sir John, 53, 76
Histoire des Chênes, etc. See Michaux
History of English Gardening. See Johnson, George W.
Holland, Lady, 146
Holland, Lord, 146
Holly (evergreen), 46, 83
Hollyhocks, 151
Hood, William, 36
Hortense, Queen, 132
Hortus Britanno-Americanus. See Catesby
Hortus Kewensis. See Aiton
Hospital of La Charité, 54

FLORALIA *Index*

Houston, Dr. William, *G. aculeata* first brought to England by, 143
Hoxton, Fairchild's garden at, 40
Hume, Sir Abraham, shrubs imported by, 147
Hunt, Francis, 36
Hunt, Samuel, 36
Huysum, von, Dutch painter, 40, 128

I*chnographia Rustica. See* Switzer
Illustration, floral, 126-27
Imperial Park of Tsar Koe-Selo, 34
Indian corn, 70
Indian Flora, 67
Indians, 70, 81, 82, 85
Iris, 150

Jamaica, 55, 69, 99, 140
James, John, 36
James, Moses, 36
James, Robert. *See* Petre
Jefferson, Thomas, 80
Joan, Queen of Sicily, 155
Johnson, Dr., on Shenstone's garden, 28
Johnson, George W., 6, 15; *History of English Gardening*, 23; on Miller, 45; on William Sherard, 52
Josephine, Empress, 132, 133, 134, 146
Juniper (evergreen), 46

Kaempfer, on camellias, 148
Kalm, Peter, 108; description of English gardens, 11; and John Bartram, 78; *Travels in North America*, 78; attitude towards America, 78-79
Kalmia latifolia (mountain laurel), 11, 46, 93
Kamel, Father Georges Joseph, 148
Kennion, Edward, *Essay on Trees, etc.*, 98-99; trips to Jamaica, 99
Kensington Gardens, dead trees placed in, 27; nursery founded by Furber, 41
Kent, William, 25, 52; and natural gardens, 20, 26-27; influence of Spenser on, 26; compared with Brown, 30
Kew Gardens, 115, 138, 141; founded, 15; George III interested in, 16; Chinese influence in, 24
Kidd, Colonel, and Calcutta Botanic Garden, 67

Kilburn, William, artist, 122
Kip, artist, 32
Koenig, Dr. John, student of Indian Flora, 67; as collector for Sir Joseph Banks, 143

Lady's slippers, 75
Lambeth Marsh. *See* Curtis, William
Lancaster, Duke of, 155
Landscape gardening, natural style of, 17; in England, 19-34
Landscape School, 24
Larch tree, 58
Laurustinus (evergreen), 46
Lawrance, Mary, *Collection of Roses*, 157, 158
Lawrence, Rev. John, 8; *Fruit Garden Kalendar*, 9
Lawson, John, *New Voyage to Carolina, etc.*, 81-83
Leasowes, Shenstone's estate at, 27; mentioned by Whateley, 29
Le Blon, James Christopher, inventor of three-color system, 126
L'Ecole Inconographie des Plantes, 131
Lectures on Botany. See Curtis, William
Leeds, Duke of, 12
Legg, John, friend of Curtis, 111
Le Nôtre, André, 20, 32, 34; director of gardens at Versailles, 19
Leo X, 155
Les Liliacées. See Redouté
Les Roses. See Redouté
Leydon, 5, 77, 80
L'Héritier, Redouté's work with, 130
Licorice, 105
Lilies, 75, 81, 147
Lindley, Dr. John, *Rosarum Monographia*, 160-62
Linnaeus, Charles, 40, 47, 50, 54, 67, 73, 74, 77, 78, 80, 89, 97, 107, 108, 120, 121, 123, 139, 143, 146, 148, 159; parents, 1; early love of gardening, 1; education, 2-4; influence of Tournefort's works on, 3; University of Upsala, 3; as professor's assistant, 3; influence of Celsius on, 4; trip to Lapland, 4; M.D. degree, 5; *Flora Lapponica*, 5; *Systema Naturae*, 5; practice of medicine, 5; as professor, 5; knighted (Carl von Linné), 5; *Genera Plantarum*, 5; sexual system of plant classification, 5; death, 6; influence, 6; correspondence with Col-

FLORALIA *Index*

Linnaeus, Charles (*Continued*) linson, 14; herbarium, 17; on Miller's *Gardener's Dictionary*, 48; visit to Sloane, 59; *Species Plantarum*, 104; imported camellias, 149; received first tea plant, 150
Linnaeus, Christina Broderson, 1
Linnaeus, Nils, 1, 2, 3
Linné, Carl von. *See* Linnaeus
Linnean Society, 17, 123
Linnean system, 47, 79, 104, 106, 107, 108, 120, 138, 139, 142
Linnhult, Sweden, 1
Lobelia, 142
Locke, John, interest in horticulture, 20
Logan, James, correspondent of Bartram, 76; as essayist, 77
London, Bishop of, 41; garden at Fulham, 39
London, horticulturist, 10
Loten, John Gideon, Esq., Curtis dedicates book to, 120
Loudon, on Whateley, 28
Louis, XIV, 19
Louis XVI, 131
Louis XVIII, 132
Louis Philippe, 132
Lowe, Obadiah, 35
Lupines, 130
Luxembourg, Redouté's painting of portraits at, 128
Lyons, Israel, Joseph Bank's interest in, 62

Madder, 105
Magazines, flower, 123
Magnol, Duhamel mentions, 107
Magnolias, 81; *Magnolia grandiflora*, 76, 151; *Magnolia altissima*, 94-95, 101, 102; *Magnolia fuscata*, 147
Malpighi, Italian botanist, 6
Mandeville, Sir John, 152
Maples, red-flowering, 81
Marie Antoinette, 34, 131, 132
Marigolds, 151
Marlborough, Duke of, 53
Marshall, Humphry, 109; *Arbustrum Americanum*, 102, 104, 105-106; childhood and education, 102; influence of cousin, John Bartram, 103
Marshallton, botanic garden at, 103
Martyn, Thomas, 16, 46; on Miller's *Dictionary*, 48
Mason, attitude towards formal gardens, 32

Masson, Francis, work under Aiton, 66; as Joseph Banks' collector, 141-42
Mawe, Thomas, Duke of Leed's gardener, 12
Maxon, William, on Walter's *Flora Caroliniana*, 91
May-apples, 81
Mezzotints, 97, 126
Michaux, André, 91; early publications, 92; diary, 92-93; *Histoire des Chênes de l'Amérique*, 107-8
Michaux, F. André, 93, 133
Miller, Charles, as curator, 16
Miller, Philip, 36, 59, 75, 76, 138, 140, 145; curator of Chelsea Botanic Garden, 15, 40, 46; *Gardener's and Florist's Dictionary*, 42, 46, 47-48, 49, 108, 148; esteem in which he was held, 45; on camellias, 149; *Gardener's Kalendar*, etc., 49; birth, 49; a contemporary on, 49-50
Milton, Mr., engraver, 122
Mitchell, Dr. John, Virginia botanist, 81
Mitford, William, Gilpin's dedication to, 97
"Mock-Bird," 87
Moira, in Ireland, garden of Rawdon at, 52
Monardes, Dr. Nicol, *De Rosa et partibus ejus*, 156
Montagu, Mrs. Elizabeth, 54
Montagu, Lady Mary Wortley, 13
Montpelier, Locke's stay at, 20
Morrison, botanical system of, 107
Mosses, 75
Museum of Natural History, work of Redouté in, 131, 136
Myrtles, 80

Napoleon, interest in Redouté's *Les Liliacées*, 133
Narcissus, 49
Natural History. *See* Catesby
Natural History Museum, South Kensington, 65
Naturalistic School, of gardening, 20, 29, 30
Nelson, David, gardener, 67
Newfoundland, Joseph Banks' scientific expedition to, 63
Newton, Sir Isaac, 60
Nicholson, Lieutenant General F., 84, 87
Northumberland, Duke of, 150

FLORALIA *Index*

Oaks, 81, 83, 96, 98, 101, 107-8
Ogeche lime tree, 104-5
Orchids, 142
Orléans, Gaston d', 130
Orléans, Princess Louise d', 132, 135
Orléans, Princess Marie d', 132, 135
Otaheite, 65, 68
Oxford Physic Garden, first English greenhouse in, 10

Pacoons, 81
Palmetto tree, 102
Pansies, 150
Parkinson, and Curtis, 111
Parlyon, Monsieur, chemical professor, 55
Parsley, cow, 114; fool's, 115
Payne, publisher of Burnaby's *Travels, etc.*, 80
"Pease," 11
Pembroke, Earl of, 37; gardens at Wilton, 53
Persian date palm, 67
Peruvian Bark, 105-6
Petit Trianon, 34, 131
Petiver, James, apothecary, 147, 150
Petre, Lord, 75, 87; experiments with greenhouse plants, 148-49
Phillyrea (evergreen), 46
Physique des Arbres. See Duhamel
Pineapple, early cultivation of, 13
Pitcairn, Dr. Gulielmo, as gardener, 53; Walter dedicates *Flora Caroliniana* to, 91
Plants, sexuality of, 40; circulatory system of, 40; "Domestick," 42; scientific classification of, 67
Plates, copper, Miller's *Dictionary* illustrated with, 47
Pliny, 161
Plot, garden designer, 32
Pope, 20, 25; article in *Guardian* on gardening, 21-23; garden of, 24
Poplars, flowering, 81
Portland, Duchess of, 53-54
Price, Sir Uvedale, 34; on Brown, 31
"Providence," 69
Pultney, Dr., herbarium, 17; on Miller, 50
Pyracantha (evergreen), 46

Raphael of Flowers. *See* Redouté
Rashult, Sweden, 1
Rawdon, Sir Arthur, influenced by Sherards, 52

Ray, John, George Johnson on, 6-7; and Sloane, 45, 54, 56; botanic system of, 107
Red-birds, 81
"Red flowering lillies," 75
Redouté, Antoine-Ferdinand, 129
Redouté, Pierre Joseph, 108, 126; birth and education, 127-28; travel and study in Flanders and Holland, 128; work with André, 128; portrait painting, 128; in Paris, 128-29; work with brother, 129; interest in pastoral scenes, 129; study of botany, 129-30; influence of L'Héritier, 130-31; and Van Spaendonck, 130-31; fame, 131; and Marie Antoinette, 131; as teacher, 131-32; inventor of new method of color engraving, 131, 132; attitude towards flowers, 132; volumes illustrated, 132-33, 136; *Les Liliacées*, 133, 134; publications, 133, 134, 135, 136; *Les Roses*, 134-35, 162, 163; quality of work, 136-37; death, 137
Relhan, herbarium of, 17
Repository. See Andrews
Repton, Humphrey, as garden designer, 32; as author, 33
Revesby Abby, Joseph Banks' country place, 64
Rhododendron, 140
Rhubarb, 105
Rivington, C., printer for Miller's *Dictionary*, 47
Roberg, Professor Lars, 3
Rockley, Mrs. Cecil, on English gardening, 31-32
Rogers, John, on Miller's *Dictionary*, 48
Rose, a gardener, 13
Roses, 152-63; cabbage, 135; *centifolia*, 135; York, 135; Lancaster, 135; *Le Rosier de Lady Banks*, 135
Roses, books on, 133-34, 135
Rossig, *Roses Drawn and Coloured After Nature*, 156; *Die Rosen*, 157
Rothmann, Dr. John, influence on Linnaeus, 2, 3
Rousseau, Jean Jacques, writings on rural life, 27; *La Botanique*, 133, 136
Roxburgh, Dr. William, student of Indian Flora, 67
Royal Academy of Sciences, 107
Royal College of Physicians, 55
Royal Garden of Plants, in Paris, 54; in Madrid, 146

FLORALIA Index

Royal Horticultural Society of London, 124, 162
Royal Society, 49, 55, 56, 59, 60, 63, 64, 66, 84, 89, 107, 160; makes Bradley a Fellow, 8; makes Duilhier a Fellow, 9; purpose and influence, 17, 38; plants presented to, 47
Royal Society of Berlin, 60; of Upsala, 79
Rudbeck, Professor Olaud, 3
Rutland, Duke of, 9

Sago palm, 67
St. Hubert, birthplace of Redouté, 127
Sandwich, Lord, and Joseph Banks, 64
Sandys, traveler, 153
San-Sa-Tsubaki. See Camellias
Sansom, F., 121, 122, 124
Sarracenia, 87, 141
Sassafras, 70, 81, 102
Schuylkill River, 14, 73, 76
Scilla siberica, 146
Sea kale. See *Crambe maritima*
Sexual system of plant classification, 5, 77, 80. See *also* Linnean system
Shenstone, William, 31, 64; as foremost exponent of picturesque gardening, 27-28
Sherard, Dr. James, garden at Eltham, 52; brought plants from Germany, 144
Sherard, Dr. William, patron of exotic botany, 52; and Catesby, 83-84; founded botanical professorship, 111; brought plants from Jamaica, 140
Sibthorp, Dr., 62, 76, 111
Siddings, Mr., on formal gardens, 32
Sims, Dr. John, 160; *Annals of Botany,* 156
Singleton, George, 36
Sloane, Sir Hans, 53-54, 66, 84, 102; and Botanic Garden at Chelsea, 15, 45-46; Miller's *Dictionary* inscribed to, 47; and Miller, 50; and Duchess of Portland, 53; birth, 54; founder of British Museum, 54; education, 54-55; honors received, 55, 60; trip to West Indies, 55-56; published *Catalogus Plantarum, etc.,* 56; Oxford degree, 56; physician and botanist, 57; collections, 57-58, 60; letter from Goodricke, 58-59; purchase of Chelsea Physick Garden, 59; visit of Linnaeus to, 59; death, 59; will, 61; correspondence with Bartram, 76
Småland, Sweden, 1
Smith, Sir James, Linnean Society established by, 17; author of *English Botany,* 123
Society of Apothecaries, 114
Society of Friends, 104
Society of Gardeners, 94, 138; Miller a member of, 15; *Catalogus Plantarum,* 15, 36-40, 42, 51-52; members of, 35
Solander, Dr., on 'Endeavour" with Banks, 64, 65; as correspondent of Bartram, 76
Sowerby, James, designer of plates for Curtis's book, 120, 122; and for Dr. Smith's *English Botany,* 123, 124
Spaendonck, Gérard van, 130
Species Plantarum. See Linnaeus
Spectator, 21
Speechley, William, contribution to English horticulture, 12, 13
Spencer, William, 36
Spenser, 26
Stoves, for plants, 12, 42, 47, 95, 123, 149; for "Exoticks," 38
Sugar trees, 80
Sun flowers, 151
Sweet, Robert, named roses for Miss Lawrance, 158
Sweet potato, 70
Switzer, Stephen, interest in gardening, 10-11, 24, 25; *Ichnographia Rustica,* 11
Sydenham, Dr. Thomas, Sloane recommended by, 55
Systema Naturae. See Linnaeus

Talleyrand, 133
Talwin, Thomas, Curtis at home of, 112
Tea plant, 105, 150
Thompson, John, 36
Thornton, Dr. John Robert, observation on Curtis's and Smith's botanical works, 123; encouragement of exotic botany as Clapham, 139
Thornton-Hall, "Exoticks" raised by Lord Petre at, 149
Thory, C. A., text of Redouté's *Les Roses* written by, 134; on J. Lindsley, 162, 163
Thunberg, 66, 142; *Flora Japonica,* 150

186

FLORALIA *Index*

Tiliander, 1
Tomsbodo, Sweden, 1
Tornaco, Princess of, 128
Torrey, Dr. John, on Dr. Colden, 79
Tournefort, 6, 107; *Elémens de botanique*, 3; Miller a pupil of, 47; and Sloane, 54-55
Travels in North America. See Kalm
Trees, American, catalogue of, 106-7
Trees, books on, 12, 13, 94-109
Trillium, pink, 87
Trumpet flower, 87
Tsar Koe-Selo. See Imperial Park
Tulips, 49
Tyler, Johannes, and copper plates, 126

Ulrica, Queen of Sweden, 72, 73
Umbrella plants, 81
Upsala, University of, Linnaeus at, 3; Linnaeus a professor in, 5; botanical garden of, 13
Uvedale, Dr., collection of, 53

Vaux, Dr. George, Curtis in home of, 112
Ventenat, Redouté's illustrations in works of, 132, 133
Verney, Monsieur du, lecturer in Anatomy, 55
Versailles, 19
Vilvorde, Redouté at, 128
Violet, bird's foot, 140
Virgin's-bower, 147

Walker, Dr., founder of Cambridge Botanical Garden, 16
Walpole, Horace, 32; "Essay on Modern Gardening," 25; on Kent, 26
Walpole, Sir Robert, 53

Walter, Thomas, 109; *Flora Caroliniana*, 90, 91, 141
Wangenheim, Friedrich Adam Julius von, 106, 109
Washington, George, and "Haw, Ha!" 26
Watteau, 129
Watts, Mr., Sloane on, 45
Wavell, Mr., partner of Curtis, 113
Welstead, William, 36
West Indies, 55, 68, 69, 143
Weston, Richard, 105; on garden calendars, 95-96
Wexicoe, Latin school at, 2
Whateley, on Shenstone's garden, 28; *Observations on Modern Gardening*, 28-29
White, Rev. Gilbert, 114
White, Thomas, 114
Whitmill, Benjamin, 36
Whortleberries, 140
Wilton, Earl of Pembroke's gardens at, 53
Winch, herbarium of, 17
Wise, Switzer and, 10
Woodward, herbarium of, 17
Worshipful Company of Apothecaries, given garden by Sloane, 45; Miller's *Dictionary* dedicated to, 46

Yapon. See youpon
Yellow jasmines, 81
Yew (evergreen), 46
York, Duke of, 155
Young, William, gardenia named for, 143
Youpon, 83, 102

Zizyphus lotus, 58

www.ingramcontent.com/pod-product-compliance
Lightning Source LLC
Chambersburg PA
CBHW021123300426
44113CB00006B/271